Derby Unco

Compendium

Handpicked articles from Issues 1 to 6 of the

Derby Uncovered Newspaper

Volume 1

www.derbyuncovered.com

www.facebook.com/derbyuncovered

www.instagram.com/derbyuncovered

First published in 2023

Derby Uncovered Group
76 Bramfield Avenue
Derby, Derbyshire, DE22 3TL
www.derbyuncovered.com

Introduction.

One of the greatest pleasures of working for Derby Uncovered is the privilege of being able to share some of the incredible stories from the wonderful history of Derby and its surrounds.

Each and every time we do, we try to make sure that its presented in a fun and enjoyable way and doesn't drown the reader in academia – for us history should be fun.

So far – judging by the incredibly kind comments we are lucky enough to receive - it's an approach that seems to be appreciated.

This book is a collection of handpicked stories from Issues 1 to 6 of the Derby Uncovered Newspaper – or as we've termed it, a compendium.

We hope that the articles we've chosen here offer a little something for everyone, and combined give a great example of just how wondrous our local history is.

David Turner
DERBY UNCOVERED and DERBY UNCOVERED CIC

This book has been very kindly sponsored by
Ashmere Care Homes.

Index

Issue 1 - The Great Flood of Derby - When the weather overwhelmed the town centre.

Derby has, over the years, experienced many extreme weather events, indeed it has been recorded that substantial flooding was experienced in Derby on many occasions such as in 1673 and 1740 and also 1750, when it was reported that Derby had, "one of the most terrible tempests of lightning, thunder and rain that was ever known." There was also the flood of 1842 which hit Derby so badly that a huge culvert had been built afterwards on Markeaton Brook, in an attempt to prevent a similar flood. However, in 1932 a flood overwhelmed those defences so dramatically that it became known as The Great Flood of Derby.

Although for a few days prior to Sunday May 22 of that year Derby had seen rather a lot of heavy rain there was, as described at the time, "no reason to anticipate the inundation that followed." An inundation came however, and at speed, with "an avalanche of water such as human ingenuity was powerless to control."

Derby in Flood, May 22nd, 1932 (Sadler Gate).
Sadler Gate during the flood.

As the waters in Markeaton Brook entered the town of Derby it passed by St. John's Church and moved along Brook Walk until it approached Ford Street. It was here that the culvert had been built ninety years previously in the hope of avoiding another large flood. Though it had so far served its purpose admirably on this occasion, "so great was the volume of water that it was now impossible to find a passage." With the water unable to pass under the bridge it had nowhere else to go apart from pouring into the streets. Once this began the sheer speed of the flood was terrifying. It was said at the time that in "the low-lying parts of the town it gathered quickly, and by ten o'clock on this Sunday morning, shops in the Corn Market, St. James's Street, and the bottom end of St. Peter's Street were immersed halfway up the windows." Flood markers had been placed on various places after the flood of 1842 to mark the height of that flood, and these were also covered making it Derby's biggest ever flood. The centre of town was described as presenting "the appearance of a lake, and the sight was unforgettable."

The electricity supply failed, as did the telephone service and the "town was soon in a plight that it had never imagined possible" as the "water swirled in the streets, twisting and tearing up road surfaces, broke plate-glass windows, poured into basements and ground floors of the shops and stores, and swept into banks and municipal offices, spreading damage everywhere." The damage wasn't restricted to the Sunday either, as damage cause by the flood that day caused an explosion the following day at H. Samuel's in the Cornmarket. The shutters and windows were blown into the street with ten people requiring treatment at the Derbyshire Royal Infirmary, "whilst the police had a busy time collecting the watches and jewellery."

The Wardwick during the flood.

Although the water receded almost as quickly as it had risen the trail of damage, both physical and financial, that it had left behind it didn't. It was estimated that the damage done to property was to the value of around £400,000, around £21.5 million in today's money. Tradespeople suffered heavily in terms of the value of individual losses, but it was the residents in the poorer districts who suffered the most and "in some cases had lost their all." These were of course the people who were least likely to have any form of insurance. Those who lived close to the brook were of course hit very hard and it was described as a "scene of desolation in the congested areas bordering upon the course of the Markeaton Brook. Willow Row, Nuns Street, Brook Street and St. John's Terrace were hit particularly hard with the inhabitants of Willow Row unable to leave their bedrooms."

The front cover of the fundraising booklet created after the flood.

A relief fund was set up at the time by the Mayor – W.H. Salisbury - with the intent of raising a money for the worst victims. As part of that fund a "Souvenir of the Derby Floods", booklet was released and available to purchase for 6d. It's from that very booklet that the quoted information in this article is from in fact. Perhaps what also makes this flood all the more striking is that it was the first that was ever photographed, allowing us to gain a sense of perspective visually – though hopefully we will never have to take our smartphones out to record another one.

Issue 1 - The Midland Drapery - The Magnet that Draws the People

When people reminisce about things long-gone there's often two particular themes that crop up. Old pubs is one of them and old shops is the other, and when old shops are mentioned in relation to Derby then more often that not we often hear of Ranby's, Barlow and Taylor's, Thurman and Malin's and of course the Midland Drapery. As the very first purpose built independent department store in Derby, the Midland Drapery, and all talk of it, brings back a lot of fond memories for some people. For myself, though too young to personally remember it, I do remember my parents talking fondly of it.

Established in 1882 on St. Peter's Street with the East Street development coming in 1892, it was described at the time as "a delight to the eye - within its doors was a well fitted and special apartment devoted to children's coats, capes, costumes, ladies underclothing and corsets". All in all, as well as its presence on St. Peter's Street, the shop occupied numbers 1-9 East Street, number 3 being the men's wear department, stocking hosiery, pants, vests, shirts in wool, collars and cuffs, ties, caps, rugs and umbrellas, and by 1909 the shop employed over 300 people and its founder and owner, Edwin Ann, was locally regarded as a very considerate employer, often organising company events to places such as Chatsworth.

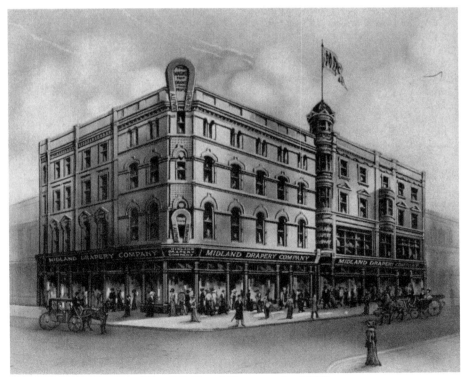

The Midland Drapery in 1887.

Displayed high on the store's frontage was its trademark magnet sign declaring the company slogan of "The Magnet that Draws the People", and it not only did but it also left them with very happy memories. On our Facebook page Patricia Shreeve said, "I loved this shop, it was a joy to wander round and the yearly visit to see Santa was magical." Frances Lilley mentions that she "used to love the restaurant in the 60s - the hairdressing salon was above with a staircase into the dining area. Freshly coiffured ladies had all eyes on them as they descended ... quite an ordeal! The adjoining Sun Lounge was great too for lighter refreshments ... loved an Ice cream sundae as a treat." Fay Slingsby, the Great Granddaughter of the stores founder – Sir Edwin Ann – remembers "being taken to lunch in the Café/Restaurant and models would intermingle among the tables showing off the latest fashions!" and agrees that "the Santa's grotto was indeed a legendary experience."

The Hosiery and Gloves Department in the Midland Drapery.

Although beginning its life as a drapery, by the 1920s it had become a true department store and drew many people in with the sumptuous and wide selection and even now, over 50 years after its closure in 1969, it's still sadly missed by many Derbeians. There's very much a universal opinion on its closure with Maxwell Craven, describing the Audley Centre that replaced it as "a bland two-storey brick shopping arcade of dubious fiscal viability" and Stephanie Brown putting it rather aptly on our Facebook page when she said, "We lost such an iconic store for the crappiest of crap Audley Centre which had to be one of the most depressing buildings in Derby!". As with many things of that era it fell victim to what was perceived at the time as progress and it's doubtful whether such a magnificent building would have been demolished in these times, but demolished it was and Derby was the poorer for it.

The Arcade looking East in the Midland Drapery.

We hope, as we do with everything that we do at Derby Uncovered, that these pictures will bring back some fond memories for many of you and as with everything that we do, we'd love to hear from you if you have your own memories or pictures that you'd like to share.

Issue 2 - Friar Gate Bridge. - What is the next stop for this iconic landmark?

I've been interested in our local history now for almost 30 years, but the other month a conversation I was having made me pause and ponder a question – what was it that first triggered the interest? Reaching back over the years I realised it was my memories of both Friar Gate and also Friar Gate Bridge.

As a young child we didn't really venture far up Friar Gate that regularly. Pickford's House Museum wasn't opened until 1988 and our visits to the town centre were based around the Eagle Centre and its surrounds. It would be, for example, on the occasions that I had a doctor's appointment on Vernon Street, that afterwards myself and my mother would stroll down Friar Gate into town.

Friar Gate Bridge, Derby

Each time we did, three things would always stand out for me. The first was a childlike wonder at the, what seemed to me at the time, huge step-down kerbs. The second was the magnificence of many of the buildings on the street.

The third was Friar Gate Bridge and it was a combination of these things that first stirred my interest into what Derby had once been like.

For many people the bridge is one of the most iconic Derby landmarks. It appears in many paintings and pictures and it certainly has a very special place in our city's legacy.

In just five years the bridge will be 150 years old. It was built in 1878 by Andrew Handyside and Company, a Derby-based iron foundry firm and was designated a Grade II listed structure in 1974. If you look around at the surrounds of Friar Gate and picture the elegant houses at the time of its erection, you won't find it hard to imagine that a simple plate girder bridge would have been considered unsuitable for such a location. Instead, Friar Gate Bridge was designed with an elegant arch in cast iron, with moulded parapets and spandrels incorporating the town's 'buck-in-the-park 'emblem.

It was this bridge with its elegant arches that served as the inspiration for the 1932 song 'Underneath the Arches '- one of the most famous songs of the duo Flanagan and Allen. In 1957 Bud Flanagan told the story of how he had written the song in Derby in 1927, with its references to the arches of Derby's Friar Gate Railway Bridge and to the street homeless men who slept there during the Great Depression

Friar Gate Bridge c.1908.

The bridge became redundant in 1968 when, as part of the Beeching Report - a plan that intended to increase the efficiency of the nationalised railway system in Great Britain - the railway line closed. In the early 1970s the adjoining viaduct to the north-east was demolished and it seemed that the bridge itself might follow suit. It was passionate public support for the survival of the bridge that led to its Grade II listing.

In 1985 the bridge was purchased by Derby City Council from British Rail for the sum of £1 and alongside that purchase came the obligation to maintain it. Though sporadic painting has been carried out alongside some cosmetic restorations, the drainage of the bridge remains poor, it suffers from widespread corrosion and it is now covered in safety netting.

Thankfully for the citizens of Derby the bridge has an organisation fighting for its future – the Friends of Friar Gate Bridge (FFGB).

In 2015, The Friends of Friar Gate Bridge was established to provide a single, recognised organisation for the public to channel their concerns over the condition of the bridge. For decades successive Council administrations had failed to treat the restoration of the bridge as a priority, despite their legal obligation to maintain it, but The Friends now have an ongoing dialogue with councillors and officers which keeps the bridge in focus. The Council has many serious challenges in trying to meet its wide range of responsibilities and no one expects it to find all the funds required to restore the bridge properly. Nevertheless, there is now a constant awareness that the bridge needs to be dealt with and, among other things, the Council submitted an application to the Government's Levelling Up Fund for the bridge's restoration (the result being due in January 2023).

Financed by Heritage Lottery, in 2018, the Friends commissioned a report from Latham's Architects on the viability of various future uses for the bridge. While standalone developments were seen as possible, the likely most viable solution would involve any future economic activity being linked to developments on the adjacent Goods Yard site. Subsequently, the Friends organised a meeting with the Council, Clowes Developments (owners of the Goods Yard) and Derby University to discuss possibilities. Although set back by both the Covid pandemic and the current economic climate, dialogue has continued with these parties and a plan is steadily emerging. It may be a few more years before the bridge is restored but the Friends are confident it will be.

Issue 2 - The Derby Pyclet - Hundreds of years of history in a tasty mouthful.

Derby has a few interesting claims when it comes to the world of food. Harry Stevens – the inventor of the hot dog – was born in Litchurch, Derby and Matthew Walker's Famous Christmas Puddings trace their origins to 'a humble Derbyshire farmer's son all the way back in 1899'. Surely though, when it comes to a food that lays claim to the longest roots in our local history, it must be the unique Derby pyclet. What's even more remarkable is that at one point it even disappeared from existence – only to make a stunning comeback.

With a history that can be traced back to Saxon times, the Derby pyclet was originally sold in the city of Derby all the way back in 1864 when we were a mere town. It was sold by the Monk family with the opening of their new pyclet bakery on the corner of Edward Street and North Parade. Whilst the men baked, the women sold the pyclets from barrows under the Guildhall arch in Derby.

A recoloured picture of Emily Monk under the Guildhall arch in Derby.

Emily Monk took her place behind the barrow in 1914. In her own words she was to remain there 'everyday bar high days and holidays' until 1963. Upon Emily's passing she was succeeded by a lady called Rose - who lived next door to the bakery and had, for many years, helped the family.

It was a combination of factors that led to the demise of the Derby pyclet in 1973. With the rise of the supermarkets and the oil crisis playing a part, alongside the lack of desire from the younger members of the family, the end result was production of the Derby pyclet ceasing with the pyclet bakery being split into four houses the following year.

The Derby pyclet and all of the history and tradition behind it was, in all practicality, gone for ever. Or was it? Some things aren't meant to be over though and in 2011, when Mark Hughes bought his first home, the rebirth of the Derby pyclet began.

Mark's first home just happened to be a converted shop and when his conveyancing solicitor recognised the name Monk on the deeds, he recalled their history. By June 21 that year, and after some experimentation, a recipe that bought the Derby pyclet back to life was created. After wowing friends with the new pyclets at a party, the next stop was to turn up to Derby Market Hall the following month with a pop-up. With the pyclets proving to be a roaring success they found themselves ready to move into a bespoke bakery inside the Market Hall itself.

After four successful years in the Market Hall, it was time for Mark to pass on the reigns and the ownership changed hands, this time to the immensely capable hands of Katie Gibson – the current business owner.

Katie herself had been introduced to pyclets in 2016. After falling in love with them after she had stopped at the Pyclet Parlour with her sister for lunch, Katie became a regular and the parlour became her favourite lunch break venue while working in healthcare management at the University of Derby. Over the course of six months Mark had discussed with Katie his intentions of selling the business and seeing the potential, Katie purchased it from him. On September 1, 2016 the Derby Pyclet Parlour opened under her ownership.

The delicious Derby Pyclet.

From 2016 to 2018 the Derby Pyclet Parlour served countless happy customers. People would come from far and wide to sample this unique food. One gentleman from Arizona, upon his arrival in London, drove all the way to Derby so he could eat them for breakfast.

In 2018 major renovations began at the Market Hall necessitating a move. Although their initial new location – The Post House on Victoria Street – proved unsuitable as a long-term venue, it did allow Katie to reach a new audience and subsequently from July to October of that year Katie organised a temporary relocation to 85 Stepping Lane, where numerous businesses and individuals continued to order from. Whilst here, Katie planned the opening of their newest premises – Unit 41 in the Eagle Market which was opened later that year.

New and old faces flocked to buy their pyclets and the new location was a roaring success. The only thing that hadn't been anticipated was the one thing that none of us anticipated or could be expected to – a global pandemic. When COVID-19 caused a national lockdown, the unit was closed in line with national guidance. With supermarkets struggling to find delivery slots for people, Katie and her team came to the rescue of many of them. Working 24/7 they added fruit, veg and essentials goods to their deliveries. Katie herself made the huge sacrifice of shielding for nearly 12 months while baking, alongside increased deep cleaning, PPE and contactless deliveries. In 2021, with normality somewhat beginning to resume, Katie organised a move to 12 Sadler Gate where she transformed a tired charity shop into a pyclet palace comprising of two kitchens, a dining parlour and two exquisite private dining rooms over three floors. An immediate roaring success, it was again to suffer from something that couldn't be anticipated – the sheer number of cases in the Omicron wave and the surge of COVID-19 that decimated the Christmas trade and which dragged on into the New Year.

The Derby Pyclet Parlour in the Eagle Market.

Taking it as a signal to adapt and learn, Katie took the bold step of removing two dining tables from the front of the premises and extended the kitchen to bring the baking downstairs and into the full view of the shop window, with the first-floor landing converted into a dining space and a history display placed across the front of the counter. Though a corner was turned with COVID-19, by March of 2022, the cost-of-living crisis began to emerge alongside Putin's obscene attack on Ukraine and Katie, along with many other businesses, received a new energy quote for 2022/23 that was simply unworkable. Nine months after opening, Katie took the decision to close the premises.

Don't despair though, Katie and the Derby pyclets are still very much a going concern. Katie still produces pyclets for local shops, and for click and collect and home delivery. Katie has also found time to release a book – Taste the Menu – which gives a much more in depth look at the history of the Derby pyclet as well as some delicious pyclet recipes. Oh, and for the uninitiated who maybe aren't sure what exactly a pyclet is, I think the description from the local food critic and journalist Ria Amber Tesia mentioned in Katie's book is just perfect.

"Think of it as a love-child of a sturdy crumpet and silken pancake, where opportune craters create wonderful pockets for gooey fillings (or melted butter if you are so inclined)."

My personal recommendation? Order some pyclets, and when you fall in love with them as you will inevitably do, then buy the book.

Issue 2 - S. H. Parkins - Solving the mystery of one of Derby's greatest artists.

In terms of doing my research, the difference between this version of Derby Uncovered, and the first version of Derby Uncovered back in 1998, is the same as the difference between night and day. Back then there were many trips to both Derby Local Studies Library – at that time on Iron Gate – and also to the Derbyshire Record Office in Matlock.

Whilst both are wonderful places to visit, and I'd recommend that you do, it did require a degree of planning. These days – almost twenty-five years later – we have a whole world of information at our fingertips without even leaving the house. Of course you can't always find everything you want immediately, but more often than not it is possible to at least find information on where to physically go to find it. It's rare – very rare – that you can find absolutely nothing of note even after googling extensively.

Very rare means that it must happen every now and then and this happened for me with a search for the mysterious S. H. Parkins.

To give you the full back story, in 1936 the Derby Museum and Art Gallery received a collection of over 500 paintings of various Derby scenes. The paintings were given by Alfred E. Goodey, a collector of paintings, prints and photographs, and included the work of artists such as Alfred John Keene, Ernest Townsend, Ernest Ellis Clark and C.T. Moore.

My personal favourites though always seemed to have the same signature – S. H. Parkins.

As usual, I had visited Google but each time I did I returned having gained no knowledge at all. I couldn't find a name, a date of birth or even a gender. I saw the odd mention of the name next to images of their work but that was it.

It became a part-time obsession over a few months. Every now and then I'd do a quick search hoping that something would pop up, but it never did.

But in early December 2022, that all changed.

At the time I was on a website called newspapers.com – a fascinating site with literally millions of old newspaper pages viewable online – looking for information on one of the many executions that once took place in Derby. As it often did, a thought popped into my head: "Why not do a quick search for S. H. Parkins?"

I searched with low expectations – nothing I'd previously done had ever produced any helpful information – when suddenly I saw something.

An aerial view of Derby from the Shot Tower. The tower was demolished in 1932.

It was a Derby Evening Telegraph newspaper article from October 12, 1945 with the headline: "We Forgot A Man Who Drew Forgotten Derby". It seemed as I read the article that even as far back as then, the identity of S.H. Parkins was a mystery. The article ended with an appeal to the newspaper's readers for any information they might have.

It was just four days later that the readers answered a great deal about that identity.

I learnt from the follow-up article that it was a Mr. Parkins so that was the gender solved. He had, it seemed, died around twelve years prior to the article and it went on to explain that he had moved to Derby from London in 1900. The reason for the move was for him to do 'a couple of days work' for Messrs. Bemrose and Sons, however he ended up staying there as an employee for 25 years!

Expanding further, it detailed how he had lived on Arboretum Street, and that he'd previously been the assistant editor of a Sunday paper and spent a lot of time in Paris devoting his spare hours to art. He was referred to by people who had met him as a 'very small, quiet and most lovable man' and invariably wore a silk hat and frock coat and was a 'fine old Victorian character'. It was Alfred E. Goodey himself that had commissioned him to do his paintings of Derby.

It seemed I'd gone from knowing virtually nothing to having a wealth of information and I was over the moon. One thing was still missing though, and it nagged at me – his first name. A visit to Ancestry.com soon took care of that. Armed with my newly gleaned knowledge, I soon found Mr. Parkins in the 1911 Census living at 34 Arboretum Street.

His name was Samuel. 'Nice to meet you, Samuel', I thought as I smiled.

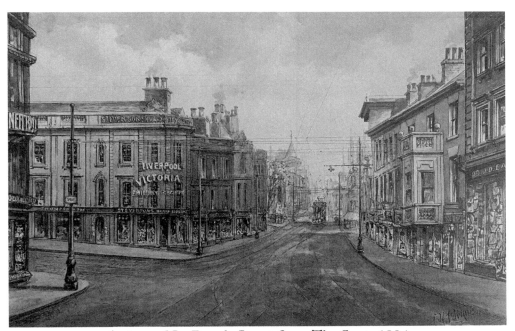

A view of St. Peter's Street from The Spot, 1924.

By the end of my searches, I knew that Samuel was born around 1849 and had lived in Marylebone, London. He had been married twice. The first marriage was to Amelia F. Parkins, who I believe died around 1887, and the second to his wife who had been living with him in Derby – Maria. She was herself from Paris, which tied into what I had read in the Derby Evening Telegraph about the time he had spent there. As well as Arboretum Street he'd also previously lived at 47 Rosehill Street.

So, there you have it – mystery solved. Or almost.

The last mystery remains as to what the H stands for. According to the 1921 Census on Find My Past it stands for Henford, but I believe it also reads as Hereford. I let you as the reader decide what you think.

And why was it so important to me to find all this out? Of course, part of it was an almost obsessive desire to solve a mystery but the other part I believe goes much deeper.

I'm a firm believer that history, especially local history, isn't just about the actual paintings and photographs – as marvellous as they are. It's about the people who made them, the people who are in them and the people who inhabited our area in times gone by. Their stories and lives are, for me at least, our true history.

Whatever your religious beliefs, or lack of, I think we all agree that you can't take anything with you when you die. What you can be, and should be, is remembered, and I'm happy that Samuel H Parkins can now be remembered.

A view looking up Babington Lane in the mid-1920s. Note that the Hunters store is yet to be built.

Oh, and one more thing. The fact that paintings like this survived in the first place is down to two things. One is, of course, the generosity of Alfred E. Goodey. The other is the sterling work done by all three of the Derby Museums – the Museum and Art Gallery, Pickford's House and the Museum of Making – to preserve our history and legacy. If you haven't visited them in a while, I'd gently suggest that you do – they are well worth a visit. Even if you have, then go again. Take a friend who hasn't done so and introduce them to the wonderful world of our local history. If you want to keep up to date with what they have going on, here are their social media links at the bottom of this page.

https://www.facebook.com/derbymuseums

https://twitter.com/derbymuseums

https://www.instagram.com/derbymuseums/

Issue 2 – Bakewell - Picturesque, historic and the home of the Bakewell Pudding.

Located in the Derbyshire Dales, Bakewell is both incredibly picturesque but also steeped in history. The market town lies on the River Wye, 13 miles south-west of Sheffield and close to both Haddon Hall and Chatsworth House – two of Derbyshire's most beautiful tourist attractions in their own right. It has long been a popular destination for tourists, both from within Derbyshire itself and also from much further afield, however many may not know just how far back its history stretches.

It was first referenced in the Anglo-Saxon Chronicles in 924 and was referred to as Badecanwiellon. By 949 it was referred to as Badecanwelle and by the time of the Domesday Book in 1086 it was known as Badequella. The name itself means a spring or stream of a woman named Badeca or Beadeca. It is thought that there may have been a Saxon by that name who settled by the warm springs which rose at Bakewell and the town was named after them. Followers of Derby Uncovered social media will have seen how this has happened in other places such as the Wardwick in Derby.

Bakewell Bridge.

By the time of the Domesday Book - a great land survey commissioned by William the Conqueror – the town already had a church, a mill and a lead mine. The church, All Saints' Church, Bakewell, was founded in 920 during Anglo-Saxon times and the churchyard is home to two 9th century Saxon crosses.

A market was established in the town in 1254. Back in that time it had very few shops, so in order to buy or sell anything, people had to go to the market. It very soon became a flourishing market town that also began to hold annual fairs in addition to the markets. Due to the increase in traffic and trade, a stone bridge was constructed in c.1300. The bridge has five arches and was widened in the 19th century. It is now Grade I listed.

All Saints' Church, Bakewell.

Hidden behind All Saints' Church in Bakewell you can find the oldest standing building in the town. Now the Old House Museum, it dates all the way back to 1534 and was originally a tax collector's cottage. During the reign of Elizabeth I, the size of the house was increased and it even had it's own garderobe - an internal Medieval toilet. In 1777 the Old House was divided into five cottages for mill workers by Richard Arkwright, founder of the modern factory system. By the 1950s the cottages were considered unfit for human habitation but were saved from demolition by the Bakewell & District Historical Society. Now, as a museum, you can explore the stories of the people who inhabited the house such as Christopher Plant, the Tudor title

19

assessor and the Pitt family who lived in one of the cottages in Victorian times. The museum is open from March 25 to November 5.

When visitors now walk around the beautiful town it might be hard to picture, but back in 1779 Bakewell was in fact the scene of a riot. The backdrop to this was the practice of the time of men being chosen randomly under the Militia Ballot Act, in which each county in the kingdom was required to send a number of men for army training. With rumours abounding that Bakewell was being asked to give more than its fair share of men, many of them, including lead miners with picks and shovels, gathered in the surrounding villages and marched into a meeting of the magistrates. Looting commenced and the magistrates called in the soldiers which resulted in six men being imprisoned and a great deal of damage being dealt to the town.

When Richard Arkwright, in 1777 leased the site that would become Lumford Mill it resulted in around 350 people, mainly women and children, being employed there and the workforce were housed in cottages. The oldest part of the mill is now a Grade II listed building.

The Rutland Arms, Bakewell.

The modern layout that we see today in the town of Bakewell, only came about in the 19th century when Rutland Square was created and the Rutland Arms replaced the Old White Horse

Inn in 1804. Jane Austen is believed to have stayed at the Rutland Arms in 1811 and it is further believed that she based the market town of 'Lambton' in Pride and Prejudice on Bakewell itself.

No mention of Bakewell would, of course, be complete though without talking about the famous Bakewell Pudding.

Bakewell Puddings - not to be confused with Bakewell Tarts - are a traditional dessert made from a flaky pastry base with a layer of sieved jam topped with a filling of egg and almond paste. It is said that they were first made accidentally in the kitchen of the Old White Horse Inn, (now the Rutland Arms). A cook was supposedly left with the instruction to cook a strawberry tart by Mrs. Greaves, the landlady at the time. The cook, instead of stirring the eggs and almond paste mixture into the pastry, spread it on top of the jam. Unexpectedly the result of her mistake was a resounding success.

Bakewell Tarts are actually a variant of the original Bakewell Pudding but whatever your preference is, the best location to purchase these desserts, which are now known worldwide, is the place from where they originated – Bakewell.

Ultimately whether its for the food, the beautiful views or the history, Bakewell is a very deserving location to put on your 'must see' list of places to visit.

Issue 3 - Condemned to death - The often brutal history of crime and punishment in Derby.

Having been interested in local history for around 30 years, I have on plenty of occasions, noticed that one part of our area's story which holds a particular fascination for many, myself included, is its history of crime and punishment. Over time Derby has seen many brutal acts of both crime and the punishment meted out for crime. Perhaps, looking from our 'modern-day' perspective, this is the reason behind our almost morbid appetite for these stories.

Derby, as with all of its history, has a long catalogue of events that happened within this sphere. For example, it can boast of having five prisons (or gaols) over time and there have been multiple executions across the centuries, often drawing huge crowds of curious onlookers.

But as we dig deeper – as we like to do at Derby Uncovered – we find even more history in these stories as we look at the lives of the condemned and the events that led up to their deaths.

The junction of St. Peter's Street and the Cornmarket – the location of Derby's first County Gaol.

The gaols included the first County Gaol that was built in the 1500s in the Cornmarket. It was built alongside the exposed Markeaton Brook which – if we recall how the majority of waste was disposed of in those days - meant that the open brook was effectively little more than the town sewer. The historian William Hutton (1723-1815) wrote that 'our ancestors erected the chief gaol in a river, exposed to damp and filth, as if they meant to drown the culprit before they hanged him'. His words were incredibly apt as in 1610 a sudden rising of the brook during the night drowned three of the captive prisoners. If you managed to avoid drowning or the hangman, then it might well be the 'gaol fever 'that got you because disease was rife inside the gaol. More than 50 prisoners died due to the insanitary conditions during a 50 year period from 1630 onwards.

For a certain period in Derby's history if you were condemned to hang then the executioner responsible for launching you into eternity would be the reviled John Crossland. Facing the death penalty himself around 1653-1658, after being accused of horse stealing, he stood in the dock alongside his elder brother and father. With Derby lacking its own official hangman, the bench perversely offered a pardon to any of the three who was prepared to hang the other two.

The father and elder brother immediately declined the offer only for John to readily accept with an *avidity* that led William Hutton to observe: *He would hang half the creation, and even the judges, rather than be a sufferer himself."* John performed the executions so well, and with such little remorse, that he became the official hangman for Derby and two or three neighbouring counties. Reviled locally for what he had done, the mere mention of his name was used to hush disobedient children – he was, in effect, the local bogeyman.

Derby's Cornmarket Gaol also once housed a prisoner who was perhaps very surprised to find himself incarcerated – John Greatorex. John was actually the gaoler who, in 1731, found himself locked up for the crime of playing football, a sport for which Mayor Isaac Borrow strongly disapproved. Declaring that 'the prison should not hold him one night', Greatorex promptly fulfilled his boast, broke out and fled before morning.

For people in Derby today the two gaols or prisons that most people would be aware of are the County Gaol on Friar Gate and its successor on Vernon Street. The gaol on Friar Gate is still partially preserved below ground level and has been turned into a fantastic visitor experience by Derby's Richard Felix and though the Vernon Street Gaol is long since gone, its stunning and historical façade still remains to this day.

Opened in 1756, the gaol on Friar Gate was designed to hold accused awaiting trials or punishment and not for punitive punishments such as incarceration for extended periods of time. Consequently, it soon became overcrowded, cramped and often lawless and it was entirely possible for felons, debtors, males, females, the young, the old, the untried and the convicted to communicate freely.

The County Gaol on Friar Gate by A. J. Keene.

It was here, in 1817, that the gaol held five men - John Brown, Thomas Jackson, George Booth, John King and Thomas Hopkinson, who were sent to trial for setting fire to hay and corn stacks.

The system of crime and punishment we had in England at that point in time is now referred to as the 'Bloody Code' - over 200 offences were punishable by death and setting fire to hay and corn stacks was one such offence.

Four of the five accused were found guilty and hanged on August 15, 1817. The exception was Thomas Hopkinson who escaped the hangman by turning King's Evidence - admitting guilt and testifying for the state.

Coming so close to the hangman, you might assume that for Thomas Hopkinson it was a lesson learnt. However, if you did assume that then you'd be very wrong.

Less than two years later, on April 2, 1819, Thomas this time kept his appointment with the hangman after being found guilty of highway robbery.

The executions themselves were often a huge public spectacle. When Samuel Bonsall, William Bland and John Hulme were executed in 1843 it was estimated that around 35,000 to 40,000 people turned up to watch, with people pouring into the town from places such as Belper and Chesterfield on specially laid-on trains organised by the North Midland Railway. With special trains laid on once more, the execution of George Smith in 1861 for the murder of his own father was reputed to have drawn an even bigger crowd still.

It's perhaps the fear of dying so publicly that made others determined to avoid the hangman at any cost. This was particularly true in the case of two brothers – John and Benjamin Jones – who in 1784 hanged themselves in their own cell rather than face their public executions. Desperate not to allow the men to escape their sentence, a doctor was summoned when the bodies were found, in a futile attempt to revive the men so they could be hanged all over again!

Opening in 1827, Derby's last gaol – at Vernon Street - was claimed to be 'one of the most complete prisons in England'. It certainly seemed that money was no object when it was built - the gaol cost £65,227 to build - around £6.6 million in today's money.

In 1833, John Leedham became the first prisoner to be publicly hanged at the gaol. John was also the last person ever to be hanged in Derbyshire for a crime other than murder. In front of a watching crowd, he was hanged for the crime of bestiality.

In 1862, the last public execution occurred in Derby and afterwards the executions took place behind the gaol walls. The condemned was Richard Thorley who, two months previously, murdered his girlfriend, Eliza Morrow, on Agard Street by slitting her throat in a jealous rage. More than 20,000 people attended the execution and afterwards his body was buried within the prison grounds.

In 1873, Benjamin Hudson was hanged for the murder of his wife in what was the first private execution to take place at the gaol. The last person to be executed at the gaol was William Slack who was executed on July 16, 1907. He was hanged by Henry Pierrepoint for the murder of Lucy Wilson in Chesterfield.

The surviving facade of the County Gaol at Vernon Street.

After the First World War the gaol acted as a military prison for prisoners who had been convicted by court martial until it was demolished in 1929. During the demolition the bodies of executed prisoners were moved into a plot of land beneath the prison walls and once the demolition was complete, only the imposing façade remained, and this can still be seen to this day.

Once demolished, a small chapter in the huge and varied history of Derby was closed.

Issue 3 - Alice Grace. - The tragic tale of 'Old Alice in the Bacon Box'.

If, as we like to believe at Derby Uncovered, the true history of any place lies in the history of the people that lived in it, and in the stories of the lives of those people, then the story of Alice Grace is both a story filled with sadness and one that deserves to be remembered – it's the true story known to some as 'Old Alice in the Bacon Box'.

Born on July 2, 1853, Alice was the daughter of stocking maker William Grace and Alice Bunting. At the time of her birth, the family lived in Holbrook and alongside Alice and her parents she also had an older brother – Joseph. By the time she was three, the family had moved to nearby Morley where Samuel and Charles became her younger siblings – born in 1856 and 1859 respectively.

Tragedy seemed to stalk the early years of Alice's life and that of her family. In 1864, at the age of only 14, Alice's older brother died. Only two years after that her youngest sibling – Charles – also died at the tragically young age of seven.

Perhaps in an attempt to start anew and leave, as best they could, the tragic memories behind, the remaining family moved to Little Eaton where they made their home on Blacksmith's Row by the Gang Road.

For Alice it seemed that no move would stop the litany of tragic and cruel events that were occurring in her life. In 1877, the now 24-year-old Alice, fell deeply in love with what she thought was the love of her life. After Alice became pregnant, her lover cruelly rejected her and many felt that this life event was the one that she never recovered from after the shock it had heaped upon her.

The tragedies kept coming – her baby daughter died in 1878 and by 1891 she had also lost both of her parents and her one remaining brother. The run-down cottage where she lived was in desperate need of improvements and Alice decided to withhold her rent in the hope of forcing her landlord to make the necessary repairs.

However, the inevitable happened and she was evicted which started her journey towards poverty and homelessness.

Though initially she attempted to live in a shed and a stable, she was forced out of both and found herself fashioning her own accommodation from an old bacon box that would have previously been used to pack sides of ham whilst using another to keep her belongings in.

Located on the canal wharf near the Clock House, sympathetic locals would sometimes provide her with food and occasionally allow her to bathe. Though attempts were made to remove her to the workhouse, she always resisted as many of the time would have done due to their fearful reputations. Cleverly, Alice would always make sure she had a sixpence on her to prove she was not destitute and she continued to work at the local paper mill for a period of time.

"OLD ALICE THE HERMIT" IN HER BACON BOX.
LITTLE EATON, DERBY.

A contemporary image of Alice Grace and her bacon box.

When she did lose her job, she survived by begging and also by telling fortunes and though the box would change occasionally, and though she moved around the village, into the quarries and on to Whitaker Lane, Alice lived this life for almost twenty years. During this time she became something of a celebrity with people coming from far and wide to see her with many taking photographs and her image was even featured on postcards.

Of course twenty years of living rough inevitably took its toll on Alice, and both her health and appearance began to deteriorate and she was eventually taken to the workhouse at Shardlow. Though two versions of how this happened exist – one being that she was too ill to resist and the other stating that she no longer had even a penny to prove that she was not destitute – it seems that all accounts agree that she actually found happiness in the workhouse and settled into a job there until her death in 1927.

It's nice to know that after a lifetime full of tragedy she finally found some happiness and peace, but the story also perhaps reminds us of the harshness of life, even in this country a relatively short time ago. Perhaps as we remember Alice and ensure that her story is never forgotten, we should also count our own blessings for what we have.

Issue 3 - Derby Midland Football Club - The story of one of Derby County's very first rivals.

As a very young - Derby County supporting – child, I would regularly look forward to my parents buying their Sunday Mirror and Sunday People so I could see if there was a match report for the previous day's game. I knew, of course, that there would be one the following day in the Derby Evening Telegraph, but there was something about the coverage of not just my team, but the entire programme of Saturday's football that appealed to me – especially in the days when most of the games were actually played on a Saturday.

As a child looking at this, from time-to-time I pondered the question as to why some cities had more than one football club while Derby only had one. Little did I realise, that for a very brief period in the late 1800s, Derby was home to another football team that was considered to be Derby's leading team – and its existence put pay to yet another local team – Derby Town FC – which had preceded them both.

Derby Midland FC actually preceded the existence of The Rams, being founded three years earlier in 1881 and both clubs share an intertwined history.

Though founded in 1881, Derby Midland FC can actually trace the very reasons for its existence back to 1844 when the Midland Railway company came into being and Derby became its headquarters. With Derby becoming home to an ever increasing number of its employees and recreational pursuits becoming more sought after, various clubs for the employees were formed.

The first club formed was the Midland Railway Cricket and Quoits Club and over the subsequent years athletics, bowls, tennis – and finally – football were added. It is perhaps ironic that, as in the case of The Rams - which was formed in 1884 as an offshoot of Derbyshire County Cricket Club - the decision to form Derby Midland Football Club was taken with a unanimous decision in a meeting on June 20, 1881 held at the pavilion of their own cricket club.

Derby Town FC – a team that could be considered by many as the trailblazers for football in Derby when it was established in 1869 – soon saw many of its players defecting to Derby Midland, including 23-year-old clerk Henry Evans who became their first captain. The defections were so widespread that within a year Derby Town FC folded.

The old saying 'what goes around comes around 'is very apt here because, three years later in 1884, the newly-formed Derby County Football Club initiated an equally ruthless raid on the

Derby Midland team's playing staff. Derby County's first two signings were Haydn Morley and George Bakewell - defectors from Derby Midland – and many more followed.

A team picture of Derby Midland FC for the 1888-1889 season.

With war effectively declared between the two clubs, they refused to play each other for three years before meeting three times during 1887-88. Though Midland won the first match, The Rams won the next two.

It was in 1888 however, that the fatal blow struck Derby Midland when Derby County, and not them, was invited to be a founding member of the Football League.

Although, alongside other rejected clubs, they struggled on and joined the Midland League for the 1889-90 season, the writing was effectively on the wall for them and in June 1891 it was announced that they had amalgamated with Derby County. In truth, the announcement was overly kind to them – they had effectively been swallowed whole with Derby County paying off their debts and taking all of their players – one of whom was Steve Bloomer. With that, the short existence of Derby Midland Football Club came to an end.

There is one more thing though. They did play against Nottingham Forest in the FA Cup in the 1889-90 season.

They won 3-0.

'Come on you Mids!'

Issue 3 - The Derby Workhouse – "Please Sir, I Want Some More..."

If we examine the entirety of his work, perhaps one of the most well-known lines quoted from any of the stories of Charles Dickens would be Oliver Twist's words in the Mudfog Workhouse " –Please Sir, I want some more…". That one line, for many, seemed to perfectly illustrate the bleak realities at that time of living within a workhouse. They certainly inspired fear in my grandma's generation – she wasn't prone to talking much about the past, at least not in my presence when I was a young child, but even long after the era of workhouses, they still instilled fear into her when she spoke of them.

In England, a workhouse was an institution where the purpose was to provide work and shelter for poverty-stricken people who had no means to support themselves. Life was very regimented, controlled and monotonous for the inmates who all wore uniforms. They rarely received visitors and could not leave unless they were formally discharged to find or take up work and provide for themselves.

If we go back to 1777, we can see that a parliamentary report records five parish workhouses in Derby - All Saints, St. Werburgh, St. Peter, St. Alkmund and St. Michael. By 1797 that number had been reduced to four with St. Michael's absent in a survey of the poor by Sir Frederic Morton Eden. The same report detailed how one house in every sixteen in Derby was an ale-house and that the workhouse with the best conditions was St. Alkmund's – with 36 people being accommodated in the workhouse - six of them under seven years old and eight of them between the ages of eight and 12.

In 1834 the Poor Law Amendment Act came into existence and took the administration of the English Poor Laws – the existing system of poor relief laws – from the individual parishes as they had been before into Poor Law Unions. Each union was an amalgamation of the existing parishes which were all now jointly responsible for the administration of poor relief in their areas - each governed by a board of guardians.

In 1837-38 the first Derby Union Workhouse was built on the south side of Osmaston Road. Designed by John Mason, it did not follow any of the Poor Law Commissioners standard plans despite the fact that the same commissioners had authorised the sum of £5,360 to be expended on the building. It served as a workhouse for just under forty years and when a new workhouse was built on Uttoxeter Road in 1876-78, the site was sold to Royal Crown Derby for a new factory.

The new Derby Union workhouse was built on the north side of Uttoxeter Road. Designed by local architects William Giles and Robert and Thomas Brookhouse, it contained a three-storey main block with a central clock tower. A central dining hall and kitchen block were contained in its rear with a chapel to the north, the infirmary to the east and a separate school building also on the north of the site. It would later become known as the Boundary House Institution, then after 1948 Manor Hospital. It was that very same hospital that, on the occasions we drove past it when I was a child, my mother and father would occasionally mention the 'old workhouses'. Manor Hospital closed in 1988 and was demolished in 1992.

The entrance to the workhouse on Uttoxeter Road, Derby.

From as early as 1914 a Poor Law Hospital – to care for the union's sick and poor – had been discussed. Though work was delayed by the First World War and its aftermath, in 1926 work finally began on the erection of the hospital on a twenty-eight acre site at the south side of Uttoxeter Road. The official laying of the foundation stones took place on June 29, 1927, with the hospital opened on November 16, 1929 by the Mayor of Derby – Alderman J.H. Grant – at a cost of £175,000. Less than six months after the opening, the Local Government Act of 1929 came into operation and control of the hospital passed to the Derby Town Council. For many years the Derby City General Hospital stood here and now the Royal Derby Hospital is situated on this site.

In 1948 The National Assistance Act abolished the last vestiges of the Poor Law and with it the workhouses, though many of the workhouse buildings were converted into retirement homes run by the local authorities. When the Act came into force an era that instilled fear into many was finally over.

Issue 3 - Death-defying daredevils! - The story of one man, a tightrope and a donkey!

When we look back into the hundreds of years of Derby's history, we can find many a strange tale. Perhaps though not many as strange as the story of one man, a tightrope and a donkey. What makes this tale so special is not just it's content though – it's the fact that we can picture it accurately as one of the key components of the story still stands today – the Cathedral tower.

Elsewhere in this issue, Mark Miley – owner of the wonderful Derbyinpictures.com website – has given us a wonderful look back at the history of Derby Cathedral and mentioned in his article that the tower was constructed between 1510 and 1530. It was this very tower in the 1700s that would play a part in the feats of not one, but two, tales of death-defying daredevils.

It is the eminent historian William Hutton, (1723-1815), who recounted in his 'History of Derby' (1791) the tale of a man named Cadman – a man he described as a 'small figure of a man' and 'seemingly composed of spirit and gristle' – who arrived in Derby in 1732 with the intent of entertaining the town by 'sliding down a rope'. We can assume from his writings on the subject that William wasn't overly impressed by such men as he states:" There are characters who had rather amuse the world, at the hazard of their lives, for a slender and precarious pittance, than follow an honest calling for an easy subsistence."

He goes on to describe how the rope in question was attached at one end to the top of the Cathedral tower – or All Saints as it was then – with the bottom end attached to St. Michaels describing it as a 'horizontal distance of eighty yards, which formed an inclined plain extremely steep'.

With a breast plate made of wood, featuring a groove to fit the rope, Cadman performed for three successive days on the rope exhibiting tricks whilst on it such as firing a pistol, blowing a trumpet, hanging from his hands and laying on his back. Though earlier showing some disdain for such shows and performances, Hutton was actually more than a little impressed and described the events as a 'wonderful exploit'.

The Cadman in question performing these stunts was in fact Robert Cadman. Born in 1711 he was an 18th century steeplejack and ropeslider who, between 1732 and 1739, performed various feats of daring. Though he escaped uninjured from his show in Derby he later died in Shrewsbury when he fell during a performance in 1739 when the rope he was using broke. He was buried at St Mary's Church in Shrewsbury, where a commemorative plaque in his memory may still be found by the west entrance.

The memorial plaque to Robert Cadman on the tower of St Mary the Virgin, Shrewsbury.

Though you might think that performance could not be outdone, Hutton then goes on to tell of a man, 'much older than the first: with a coat in dishabille; no waistcoat; shirt and shoes the worse for wear; a hat worth three-pence, exclusive of the band, which was packthread bleached by the weather; and a black string supplying the place of buttons to his waistband', who arrived in August 1734 and proceeded to tie a rope once again to the top of the tower but this time to the bottom of St. Mary's Gate.

Armed 'with a breast plate, and at each foot a lump of lead about half a hundred weight' he drew a wheelbarrow after himself with a boy of thirteen inside it from the top to the bottom, before returning to the top for one last trip down the rope – this time with a donkey!

The rope broke just twenty yards before he reached the end, and as Hutton describes it: "Legs and arms went to destruction. In this dire calamity, the ass, which maimed others, was unhurt himself, having a pavement of soft bodies to roll over". Though no-one died, 'the rope broke near the top, it brought down both chimnies and people at the other end of the street'.

Of course, these days such performances would be instantly banned – and rightly so – but it was a different world back then. Thankfully nobody – including the donkey – was seriously hurt, however the next time you're near the Cathedral tower you may find yourself glancing to the top with a slightly different perspective on things.

With centuries of history and located in the city centre itself, Derby Cathedral is a must-visit location and a location I'd highly recommend you take the time to see. If you are interested in finding out more, you can here:

https://derbycathedral.org/

https://www.facebook.com/derbycathedral/

https://www.instagram.com/derbycathedral/

Issue 4 – Shocking affair at Derby – When a star diver died in the River Derwent.

Regular readers of Derby Uncovered will remember our article in Issue 3 involving a death-defying tightrope walker and a donkey, but that was far from the only time that extremely dangerous stunts formed the basis of entertainment for the watching crowds in the town. In 1868 Mr. Thomas Worthington – a renowned and famous 'star diver – 'made his appearance at the Derby Gala for his advertised dive from 120 feet. Unlike the story in our last issue however, this stunt was to prove fatal.

Worthington captured the imagination of the public the year before when he dived from a height of 130 feet off the East Pier in Brighton. Witnessed by the King of Belgium, who in turn granted permission for the act to be performed in his home country, Worthington then proceeded to tour the United Kingdom and it was during that tour that he arrived in Derby, after extensive local promotions, to perform at the Derby Gala on May 7-9, 1868. The advertised highlight of his performance was to be a dive from 120ft.

FATAL ACCIDENT TO WORTHINGTON, THE "STAR DIVER."

A melancholy accident occurred at Derby last Thursday evening. Mr. Thomas Worthington, who has been lately performing in various parts of the country as " The Star Champion Diver of the World," was performing his feats in the Derwent, off a field belonging to Mr. Bates, of Little Chester, near Derby, in the presence of a large number of spectators, and, after going through a performance consisting of different examples of ornamental swimming, diving and floating, he came to that part of the programme setting forth "a terrific plunge in mid-air from a platform 120 feet high." Mr. Worthington mounted the platform amidst hearty cheers, and, after making various preparations, took a leap, turned one somersault while descending, attempted to turn a second, but failed to accomplish it in time, and dropped in a flat position on the surface of the river. Cries of, "It's killed him," were instantly raised, and the excited spectators waited minute by minute for his rising, but he failed to re-appear, and much excitement ensued. Mr. Smith, of Little Eaton, was one of those who jumped in after the diver, and he, on a second gallant attempt brought the unfortunate fellow to the surface dead. The body was conveyed to a tent, and afterwards to a public-house adjacent. The excitement on the ground was intense. Tidings of the occurrence quickly spread, and caused a great shock in the minds of many. The father, mother, and brother of Worthington, were present at the time of the occurrence, and were naturally greatly distressed. The deceased was rather a prepossessing young fellow, and apparently about twenty-two or twenty-three years of age.

A excerpt from a report in the Derby Mercury about the death of Thomas Worthington.

A large crowd gathered in a field on the banks of the Derwent between Derby and Darley Grove and the entertainment began from 2.20pm on May 7. Worthington, who was aged around 23, arrived at his appointed time and, in the build up to his dive, he performed a series of underwater feats including drinking milk from a bottle, peeling and eating an orange and blowing a trumpet.

At about 4.15pm Worthington began his ascent up the scaffold that had been erected and once he reached the top, he waived his handkerchief at the crowd and jumped.

Contemporary newspaper reports stated that he had turned one somersault and was attempting to turn another when he hit the water hard and on his side. Though cries of 'it's killed him' were heard from the crowd, minutes passed as people waited for him to reappear at the surface of the water. With a few people jumping into the river in an attempt to find and rescue Worthington, it was a Joseph Smith of Little Eaton, who, on his second attempt, found him and brought him to the surface.

Worthington's body was placed in a boat and taken to a tent where four local medical men, who had been visiting the Gala, attempted to resuscitate him but their efforts were in vain.

The crowd were, of course, in shock and the death was made all the more tragic because his parents and two brothers were at the event and witnessed the fatal jump.

An inquest into the death was held where the coroner returned a verdict of *accidentally drowned* and lamented that 'it was much to be regretted that there were persons ready to risk their lives in performances of this kind'.

Issue 4 - Fire at the Grand Theatre - How a fixture of Derby night life for years almost ceased to exist after six weeks.

If you take a stroll down Babington Lane these days, then on your right-hand side as you near the bottom you will come to House of Holes – an adults only crazy golf venue. For many residents of Derby, depending on their age, the building itself houses lots of memories.

Before it was home to crazy golf it was the May Sum restaurant, but it was its life before that as an entertainment venue that will bring back memories for many people. If you're around my age, you might remember it as McCluskey's, Eclipse, Ritzy, Confettis, or Tiffany's. If you're a little bit older than that, then it's memories of the Locarno ballroom that will come flooding back.

Of course, before all of these the building was home to the Grand Theatre, and this can still be clearly read on the building façade. What some of you might not know about the building, however, is that a huge fire almost made sure that none of those memories of the building would even exist.

The Grand Theatre on Babington Lane c.1912.

The theatre was designed by architect Oliver Essex for Andrew Melville and opened its doors on March 25, 1886. Described by the local press as a theatre 'of which any town might be proud', it was immediately a very popular location. The Derby Mercury stated in an article about its opening night that 'if the public continue to roll up as they did it will be found that the building is, if anything, too small'. Sadly the excitement and promise of the theatre was soon to be hit by a disastrous and tragic event less than six weeks after its opening.

On the evening of Thursday May 6, and only forty minutes before the evening performance was due to begin, a fringe overhanging a wooden scene caught fire. Alfred Whyatt, the scenic artist at the theatre, called out at once and alerted Andrew Melville who was standing in the wings. The audience at the time was thankfully quite small as the only people admitted were those who had paid for early admission – around thirty to forty people all told.

Melville initially called for the audience to stay in their seats as around ten people on the stage attempted to put out the fire. Their attempts at this proved unsuccessful with the rest of the scenery catching fire before the flames – in the words of the Derby Daily Telegraph – 'spread like lightning'.

DESTRUCTION OF THE DERBY GRAND THEATRE BY FIRE.

Immense excitement was caused in the town at seven o'clock on Thursday evening by the intelligence that Mr. Melville's Grand Theatre in Babington-lane, which was only opened to the public about six weeks since, was in flames. There was no necessity for the rumour to remain long a matter of question as the great structure is visible from many parts of the town, and within a very few minutes of the outbreak the flames were shooting through the gridiron—the highest point of the theatre—which rises above the stage.

A excerpt from a report on the fire in the Derby Mercury – May 12, 1886.

Whilst those behind the curtains made their escape the audience cleared out of the building, and though one man suffered a head injury while overcome by a fit, it was initially thought that fatalities had been avoided. This was sadly incorrect as it was later found that the blaze had ultimately claimed the lives of the actor John Adams and James Locksley, a carpenter who worked at the theatre.

As the fire consumed the building, word of what was happening spread throughout the town and a crowd of around 20,000 to 30,000 thronged to the surrounding area, inevitably hampering the efforts of the fire brigade and police. In an effort to keep the immediate area clear, around two hundred members of the 1st Derbyshire Militia – who were undergoing their annual training at the Normanton Barracks – were drafted in and the men 'rendered admirable co-operation in keeping clear the immediate vicinity of the theatre'.

By the time the blaze was finally brought under control all that remained of the theatre was its façade and side walls.

During and after the fire, much was made of the efficiency of the fire extinguishing apparatus with the Derby Daily Telegraph exonerating the Derby Brigade of all blame but noting that the water pressure itself was far too low to fight a large fire.

But what of the theatre itself? How did so many of you make so many fond memories in it under its various guises if it was destroyed by fire?

The answer, of course, is that a determined Andrew Melville had the building rebuilt even bigger and better and it reopened in November of that very same year.

Issue 4 - Noah's Ark found in Derby! - When Derby's very own Noah built his very own ark.

With two thousand years of history to draw on, it is perhaps inevitable that the annals of Derby and its surrounds contains some quirky little curiosities. Out of everything I've ever learned about our history however, surely nothing could be quirkier than the idea that Derby had its very own Noah, and he built his very own ark!

Quirky or not though it's also true – though our Noah had slightly different motives for building an ark.

Our Noah went by the name of Noah Bullock who – in the 1600s - was a citizen of Derby. Married to woman named Anna Clarke, the couple had four sons and the first three of these shared the names of the biblical Noah's sons – Shem, Ham and Japheth – and as if sharing the same name as the biblical Noah and naming his first three sons after Noah's sons wasn't enough, our Noah also built on ark.

Of course, when Noah Bullock began to build his ark on the Derwent, interest and curiosity was naturally piqued in the townsfolk. Many at the time assumed – falsely as it would turn out – that Noah's motive was either to avoid the plague which had hit Derby with a vengeance in 1665 or that he had been overcome by some sort of religious fervour.

The truth itself was much simpler than that – Noah was a counterfeiter and a clipper and needed a base where prying eyes couldn't see the illegal work he was undertaking. Counterfeiting is of course self-explanatory, but for those wondering just what a clipper did, it involved taking a small amount of metal off the edge of hand-struck coins. Over time, the precious metal clippings could be saved up and melted into bullion to be sold or used to make new coins.

Both crimes were punishable by death – hence the need for a secure base.

Though, over time, the interest in Noah died down amongst the townsfolk, the authorities remained keenly interested in just what might be happening inside the ark and in 1676 the ark was raided and Noah's nefarious crimes were exposed.

The Recorder of Derby at the time was Sir Simon Degge and it must have been expected by most that Noah would be facing the hangman's rope when he was hauled in front of him.

Sir Simon wasn't a stranger to controversy and he had even had problems with the law himself. He had been arrested as a Royalist during the Long Parliament, and after he was knighted, was twice fined by the courts for failing to do his duties. Crucially, it seemed that Sir Simon and Noah also knew each other. Some versions of events state that Sir Simon was curious as to just how good Noah's counterfeiting skills were and asked him for evidence. After being reassured that no harm would come to him if he confessed fully, Noah presented a counterfeit sixpence that was – in a very illegal sense – quite an impressive specimen.

Sir Simon was as good as his word and Noah was spared his visit with the executioner on the understanding that his ark was to be dismantled which it duly was. He died naturally some years later.

The ark itself had been moored on the Derwent close to where the Morledge is now and it is thought that the Noah's Ark pub – which was established in the 1700s – was named after our very own Noah.

The Noah's Ark pub on the Morledge, Derby.

So, the next time you're in that part of the city centre, take a look around and think about the fact that just a few hundred years ago, if you'd been looking around the same location, you'd have seen Noah Bullock of Derby's very own ark.

Issue 4 – I predict a riot! - "Violent outrages in Derby and the neighbourhood"

By the time this article is printed, it will have only been a matter of a few short days since votes were cast in local elections across the UK. Back in the 1830s however, a powder keg was developing over just who had the right to vote in the UK.

Although back then the House of Commons was populated by Members of Parliament (MPs) elected to represent constituencies as it is now, the areas covered by the constituencies had not been amended to reflect population change. This resulted in many 'rotten boroughs 'which had a very small electorate that could be used by a patron to gain unrepresentative influence within the unreformed House of Commons. At the same time some new urban centres such as Manchester had no MPs at all, and only 5% of the British population was able to cast a vote at the general election.

The Reform Bill was an attempt to address this system and when the first Reform Bill and subsequent second Reform Bill both failed to become law, the powder keg exploded with civil disturbances in many areas and all-out riots in Derby, Nottingham and Bristol.

In Derby on the evening of Saturday October 8, 1831, a crowd gathered in the Market Place eager to hear whether the second Reform Bill had been successful. At around 7pm news filtered thorough to the crowds that it had been defeated in the House of Lords.

As the numbers in the crowd slowly but substantially increased, one individual proposed that a mourning peal – traditionally sounded in the event of a death or funeral – should be rung with the bells of All Saints 'Church – now the Derby Cathedral. Unable to gain admittance to the church itself, the crowd advanced to the house of the Rev. C. S. Hope and demanded the keys which were duly delivered to them. Shortly after the bells of not just All Saints', but also St. Alkmund's and St. Peter's, commenced ringing mourning peals.

By around 10pm the number of people in the Market Place had risen alarmingly and their anger began to focus on the Market Place house and shop of William Bemrose, founder of Bemrose and Sons Ltd. William had been against the Reform Bill and had gone so far as to have a petition on display at his premises and so it was that the crowd – in the words of the Derby Mercury 'commenced an attack on the house and shop'. Missiles were thrown until every window at the front of his house had been destroyed and a Mr. Lakin – one of the constables on duty at the time – suffered a severe head injury in the melee.

A mid-19th century illustration of the Market Place.

With anger now at a fever pitch, various locations both in the town centre and further afield, found themselves under attack. The Rev. C. S. Hope's house in St. Alkmund's Churchyard was one of the objects of the crowd vengeance where, 'not only the windows, but the doors, shutters and palisades were also entirely demolished' with Markeaton Hall and Chaddesden Hall also attacked.

Overnight the crowd slowly dispersed, possibly to avoid detection as the dawn arose, but if the authorities thought that the worst of the protests were over, they were very much mistaken.

The Derby Mercury reported that by Sunday morning 'groups of persons were to be seen in every part of the town consulting upon the probability of further outrage, or witnessing the extensive injuries already sustained'. A meeting was convened at the Town Hall for 9am where the Mayor, Magistrates and 'respectable Inhabitants' met to discuss plans to restore order to the town. With the general populace then admitted, demands were made to the Mayor to release three prisoners who had been arrested the previous night during the protests. When their demands were refused, they vowed to free the prisoners themselves.

Marching from the Town Hall en masse, the protesters then walked along Friar Gate to what was now Derby's Borough Gaol – it had previously been the County Gaol but this was now located around the corner at the end of Vernon Street. Using a cast-iron lamppost as a battering ram, they broke open the door and liberated not just the three prisoners in question but a further twenty prisoners on top of that.

Emboldened by their success, the protestors then stated their intent to pull down the nearby County Gaol. The governor of the gaol was aware of what had happened around the corner and had positioned several armed men on the parapet walls in readiness for a potential attack. As the crowd of around 1,500 people advanced towards the gaol, they were warned that continuing on this course of action would result in them being fired upon, but the warnings went unheeded. Stones began to be thrown at the armed men on the parapets, and with the crowd loudly proclaiming their desire to tear the gaol down, the order was given to fire shots into the crowd. With several people also suffering from minor injuries from the volley of shots, the protest suffered its first fatality when 17-year-old John Garner was fatally wounded and died that evening of his injuries.

Though the town became 'comparatively tranquil' after this for a short period, by the time the evening came around a crowd once again started to gather in the Market Place and when the throng had again reached around 1,500 people, it moved towards the County Gaol.

By this point in the proceedings, part of a Troop of the 15th Hussars which had been stationed at Nottingham, had been summoned by the authorities and 'doubtless an influence on them', the crowd swung around suddenly to the right where they headed to Little Chester. On their arrival they unleashed their fury on the villa of a Mr. John Harrison and reduced it to a 'mass of ruins'.

Up until this point, the crowds had largely confined their rage to the property of people they believed to be inimical to the reform bill, their behaviour now became indiscriminate and few houses at the top of Iron Gate, Queen Street and King Street escaped their rage. A large number of palisades were uprooted from the outside of All Saints 'Church to be used as weapons of destruction, resulting in the Hussars patrolling the streets during the night in an attempt to prevent further disorder. During one confrontation between the rioters and the soldiers, a trooper who had been struck on the chest by a stone, discharged his rifle after pursuing the man who had thrown the missile and shot his target in the thigh.

By the time Monday came around, the authorities had hoped that the levels of anger would have died down, but this was not the case as large numbers of people began to assemble once more.

The Mayor - in a conciliatory attempt to placate the crowd – distributed handbills proposing that an address should be sent to the King and set up stalls in the Market Place for people to sign it. However the crowd was unimpressed by what was considered to be such a mild response and the stalls were soon smashed to pieces.

With the Mayor fearful of another outbreak, the Riot Act was read and the calvary charged the crowd. At this point a carbine was discharged fatally wounding John Hicking – a resident of the town.

Once the crowd had been dispersed, strong measures were taken to ensure there would be no further outbreaks of violence. Special Constables patrolled the town and at midnight on Tuesday two troops of Yeomanry arrived from Leicestershire and the danger of further outbreaks disappeared.

The following March, a number of people were tried at the Assizes for their part in the riot. Eleven of them, including one woman, were charged with breaking into the Borough Gaol. Most of them were found not guilty although two of them were sentenced to seven years' transportation for housebreaking and robbery – one of them was only 17 years old.

The Reform Bill Riots in Derby are commemorated on Friar Gate near the site of the old Borough Gaol with a series of sculpted heads. The heads represent prisoners emerging from underground cells into the light.

The Friar Gate heads – commemorating the prisoners that were released by the crowds at the Borough Gaol.

After a period of severe social and political unrest in May 1832 – known as the Days of May - the Third Reform Bill received Royal Assent on June 7, 1832, thereby becoming law. It is thought by many that this period was one of the closest times that the United Kingdom has come to a revolution.

Issue 4 - The Derby Hippodrome – "No thanks to those that have allowed this magnificent theatre to remain in its current disgraceful state – shame on you all".

Back in 1982 I was nine years old and attended Firs Estate Juniors School. As far as school life goes I had a fairly pleasant time, but some memories stand out more than others. One memory that is particularly vivid happened on the morning of October 11, 1982.

At that time anything that involved taking us out of our classroom to the room where the TV set lived was exciting, but this time it was a little bit different. We weren't being shown our usual weekly children's daytime programmes such as 'Watch' or 'How We Used To Live' – which was of course my favourite – but instead the view was of an awful lot of activity on an awful lot of water.

We had been watching the raising of the Mary Rose – a ship that had sunk all the way back in 1545 during the Battle of the Solent.

I thought back to that day only recently when I happened to be browsing one of the many Facebook pages and groups dedicated to Bygone Derby and began to read a discussion on the Derby Hippodrome. The consensus amongst some seemed to be that with the building in such a state of disrepair, it was too late to save it and the many years of history that lay within it.

For me, that couldn't be more wrong. I looked back to that day in 1982 at Firs Estate, and to me, the answer to whether the building can be saved and renovated is a resounding yes. If we can raise a ship that had sat on the bottom of the Solent for around four and a half centuries, then we can save and renovate a building that has lay in disrepair for a much shorter period.

The Hippodrome has a wonderful history that deserves to be protected and celebrated. Designed by architects Marshall and Tweedy of Newcastle upon Tyne, the Hippodrome opened on July 20, 1914 when a full-to-capacity audience watched a performance of 'September Morn'.

The location on the corner of Green Lane and Macklin Street was chosen due to its ability to attract patrons from the nearby terraced houses in Macklin Street, Becket Well Lane and Colyear Street as well as the poorer residents of nearby Little City who would save their money and visit weekly as an escape from the humdrum of their lives.

Across two periods – 1914-1930 and 1950-1959 – the theatre produced 1,158 live programmes and operated as a cinema in between. Stars such as George Formby, Flanagan and Allen, Gracie Fields, Morecambe and Wise and Frankie Howerd all performed at the theatre.

The Derby Hippodrome c.1915.

The doors closed in 1959 when the management declared the theatre to be unviable and the building was left idle until 1962 when it was purchased by the entertainment company Mecca and repurposed as a Bingo Hall. Bingo ended in 2006 and in 2007 The Hippodrome was purchased by a developer.

After Derby City Council presented an Urgent Works Order to determine the construction of the roof, the developer brought down the roof and a side wall within the auditorium, as well as the roof and the walls of the stage house. The building has remained in a state of disrepair ever since, with the building being repeatedly targeted by arsonists over the years. An especially serious fire in 2015 caused even further extensive damage.

There exists though, a core of people who are still fighting hard to promote the possibilities of saving and renovating the Hippodrome. One of those people is John Taylor.

I first managed to speak to John after being put in touch with him through a fellow lover of Derby's history and heritage – Kevin Speakman – who himself is a keen advocate of the renovation of the Hippodrome and also a thoroughly nice and helpful gentleman.

John's love of, and passion for, the Hippodrome shone through immediately. His family moved to Derby in 1928 and lived near the Hippodrome at 76 Green Lane. His grandfather, George, worked there rising from being a painter to being the front of house manager with John's father,

Tom, also a projectionist there who married usherette Elsie Hall – the both of them going on to be Mayor and Mayoress of Derby.

The Derby Hippodrome was built on the site of Green Hill House – a privately ran "lunatic asylum".

John's passion for the Hippodrome is so strong, and his knowledge so in depth, that he collated his knowledge and research into a wonderful manuscript entitled 'A Palatial Building - A short history of the Derby Hippodrome by John M. Taylor' – a manuscript so wonderful that Derby Uncovered immediately agreed to publish it later this year.

John, along with many others, shares a very similar sentiment for all those whose actions, or lack of, have contributed to the current state of the building. He, quite rightly, doesn't hold back during the introduction in his book where, after thanking various people, he wrote: "No thanks to those that have allowed this magnificent theatre to remain in it's current disgraceful state – shame on you all".

But John hasn't given up hope. Nor has Kevin Speakman. Nor have many others.

And nor have Derby Uncovered.

It is resoundingly possible to renovate and restore the Hippodrome, and what's more it should happen. Over time, the footprint of the public walking around the city centre has become ever more centred around the Derbion, and the rest of the centre is crying out for some imaginative forethought and change.

Why not have it as a venue for live music? Something the city centre has needed ever since the fire at the Assembly Rooms rendered it obsolete.

If not that, why not have it as a venue full of the works of local artists and craftspeople? We're lucky in Derby to have so many amazing artisans who could surely benefit from extra exposure.

I'm sure many of you would also have many viable ideas on how the venue and location could be used.

With effort and imagination there's no reason why the curtain can't come up once more for a brand-new dawn at the Derby Hippodrome.

Issue 5 - Death occasioned by violence – "Murder At The Derby Green Hill Lunatic Asylum"

Regular readers of our newspaper will have spotted in our last issue a mention of the Green Hill Lunatic Asylum in our article about the Derby Hippodrome. Its connection in that article was the fact that the Hippodrome was built where the asylum once stood, but in this article – and after a few requests to do so - we look a little into the history of the asylum itself and also a gruesome murder that took place there.

An article in the Derby Mercury reported that the privately run Green Hill House was Derby's first 'lunatic asylum' as the headline described the establishment.

It opened on February 1, 1832 under the superintendence of a Mr. Morris and a Mr. Fisher but for reasons unknown the partnership was short-lived and by December 5, 1832 it was reported that Mr. Morris and his wife had withdrawn from the partnership.

Though contemporary reports paint the establishment in a good light with the Derby Mercury in 1836 describing the apartments at the house as 'numerous, spacious, and lofty, affording ample space for the classification of patients', we should, perhaps, temper this with our knowledge of how patients were attended to in those times under the guise of treatment. Whatever the particulars of the treatment though, it was a murder that occurred there in 1848 that hastened the demise of the establishment.

On December 6, 1848 the Derby Mercury reported on the inquest of Samuel Tomlinson – a patient 'confined' at Green Hill House. Describing the victim's body at the inquest it was reported that 'the head presented a wretched appearance, particularly on the right side, the lower jaw being fractured, and several of the teeth knocked out'.

Tomlinson had been found in the room he slept in the night previously. The room had three bedsteads with one of them currently unused and the third slept in by another patient, Harold Strelly.

George Bailey – one of the keepers at the asylum - told the inquest that he'd left the deceased at around 7pm with Harold Strelly in their room and returned to the room at around 6.15am the following morning. He told the inquest that this was earlier than his usual time to visit the room in the morning which would have been around 7.45am.

The reason given for the early visit was that one of the patients had recently been to see him for a candle and he'd heard Samuel singing – something he was apparently prone to doing when he heard people around. On this occasion however when he heard the singing, he'd also heard an unusual noise in addition to it.

MURDER AT THE DERBY GREEN-HILL LUNATIC ASYLUM.

On Monday last, an inquest was held before Mr. WHISTON, jun., deputy Coroner for the Borough, and a highly respectable jury, at the Town-hall, on view of the body of Samuel Tomlinson, a patient confined in the Green-hill House Asylum, in Derby, and whose death took place early the Saturday morning previous.

On proceeding to view the body of the deceased, the head presented a wretched appearance, particularly on the right side, the lower jaw being fractured, and several of the teeth knocked out. The deceased was in the room where the occurrence, narrated in the evidence, took place, and in which room there were three bedsteads, upon one of which the deceased had slept the night before; one of them being unoccupied, and the third one occupied by another patient named Harold Strelly.

An excerpt from a report into the murder of Samuel Tomlinson from the Derby Mercury on 6th December 1848.

On his arrival in the room, Strelly was standing naked by the side of his own bed, with Tomlinson lying on the floor bleeding profusely and moaning. Pushing Strelly onto his bed and covering him up, he went downstairs to fetch a light and, taking with him another patient, he returned to the room where it seemed that Tomlinson was now dead. Strelly was still in his bed, unmoved from the position he'd been placed in.

George then called for Dr. Brigstock – at that time the proprietor of the asylum – and on his arrival the room was searched, and a bed lath was found with a considerable quantity of Tomlinson's blood on it. Strelly was immediately taken into the sitting room and 'secured'.

After testimony from Dr. Brigstock and Charles Borough – the visiting surgeon to the asylum – the coroner ruled that to him it was quite clear that the assailant was Strelly and the weapon was the bed lath and returned a verdict of wilful murder, with his trial to take place at the next assizes.

Strelly's trial was held the following March and during the trial he alleged abusive behaviour at the asylum, accusing Bailey of hitting him on numerous occasions. During the summing up the jury was told that there didn't appear to be any evidence that Strelly had 'wilfully committed the crime' and there had been sufficient evidence to prove his insanity at the time of the crime. If the jury agreed with this, Strelly would be sent to a place where 'he would not likely be locked up with another lunatic from 8 o'clock at night until 6 next morning, and with a tremendous bludgeon at hand."

The jury found him not guilty, on the grounds of insanity.

Issue 5 - An impatient and headstrong character - When the vicar of the now Derby Cathedral organised its demolition!

Back in Issue 3 in a wonderful piece written by Mark Miley of Derbyinpictures.com, we looked back at the history of Derby Cathedral – previously known as All Saints Church. In that piece we heard a mention of the church being demolished based on the unilateral decision of its vicar - Dr Michael Hutchinson – in order to force the Derby Corporation's hands on a new church. In this issue we look a little more into Dr Michael Hutchinson and his controversial decision.

Hutchinson had previously been the Rector of Cheadle and later the Canon of Lichfield before coming to All Saints in Derby in 1719. Prior to his arrival, the fabric of the church had begun to deteriorate and by 1700 the church was in a ruinous state. So ruinous in fact that according to Margaret Mallender, who wrote an account of the events at that time, 'people were simply afraid to attend services'. Various attempts had been made before to raise money for a rebuilding programme, including a countrywide appeal in 1714, but they had all been unsuccessful.

Derby Cathedral.

In fact, talks of rebuilding the church had been discussed for so long that to a large degree nobody took them very seriously.

Dr Michael Hutchinson took them seriously though – very seriously indeed!

Though he had no support whatsoever from the Derby Corporation for his plans, he pressed on regardless and over time collected materials that would be required in the rebuild, appointed James Gibb as the architect and appointed Smiths of Warwick as the building contractors. Sill the Corporation would not budge.

When on February 13, 1723 he made arrangements for upcoming services to be held at nearby St. Michaels, it was quite clear that he was planning something drastic.

At daybreak on February 18, 1723, workmen were secretly let into the church and were instructed to break it down. Before the citizens of the town were fully aware of what was happening, the roof was off and the walls destroyed. Only the tower – built between 1510 and 1530 – survived.

A new church now had to be built and Hutchinson was tasked with making it so.

Funds were urgently required – the contractors' estimated cost for the rebuilding was £3,250 (over £500,000 in today's money) - and a subscription list was opened to raise them. With their hands now totally forced, the Corporation gifted 200 guineas and Hutchinson himself gifted £40.

Hutchinson didn't restrict his fundraising to Derby, travelling all over England in his efforts and earning the title of 'a master in the art of begging' from the historian William Hutton. Included on the subscription list were the names of Sir Robert Walpole, the former Chancellor of the Exchequer and today often viewed as the first British Prime Minister, and Sir Isaac Newton.

For over two years – and while the church was rebuilt – services were held at St. Michaels until November 21, 1725 the first sermon in the newly rebuilt church was preached.

It was, of course. a sermon by Dr Michael Hutchinson.

Issue 5 - "I want you to believe...to believe in things that you cannot." - The night that Dracula came to town.

When Bram Stoker wrote the classic horror story 'Dracula 'in 1897 he would have never, even in his most optimistic moments, have anticipated the cultural phenomenon that would follow his tale about the evil Count.

Since it was published in 1897, Bram Stoker's Dracula has never gone out of print with the book also translated into multiple languages – ironically considering the subject matter putting it on a par with the bible in terms of popularity – and has seen over 200 movies to date featuring the Count in a major role.

Next year will also see the centenary of the stage adaptation of Dracula and its debut wasn't in the glitzy West End of London but in Derby – at the Grand Theatre on Babington Lane to be precise.

The stage play itself was written by the Irish actor and playwright Hamilton Deane and was the first authorised adaptation of Bram Stoker's 1897 novel.

In the almost 100 years that have passed since its debut on the stage, people's sensibilities have of course shifted substantially. Nowadays countless horror films are available at the mere click of a button on platforms such as Netflix, but it was a different world in 1924. So different in fact that for Dracula's initial three-night run precautionary measures were taken with a nurse patrolling the aisles to aid terror-stricken members of the audience!

The premier itself took place on Thursday May 15, 1924 - tickets would have set you back anything between 8d to 3/6 (three shillings and sixpence) - and the following day it was met with an enthusiastic review in the Derby Daily Telegraph.

Described as a 'noteworthy production' it was said that when the curtains fell just after 11pm 'half the audience were in a frenzy of applause, while the remainder were in a state of nervous prostration'.

One of the compliments paid by the newspaper succeeded in praising the production highly whilst still managing to take a dig at the horror genre generally when it said that while, 'under the spell of the breathless action and excellent acting one forgets the absolute twaddle to which one is listening. The utter drivel of were-wolves, vampires, and undead, which provokes nothing but laughter in the sane light of day, becomes dreadful reality in the awful semi-darkness of the stage.'

Derby was just the beginning of the story for the stage adaptation of Dracula. This production toured England for three years before settling in London. The Little Theatre in the Adelphi hosted the play first from February 14, 1927 with the need to accommodate larger audiences leading to it being transferred firstly to the Duke of York's Theatre and then onto the Prince of Wales Theatre.

In that very same year the play was brought to Broadway by producer Horace Liveright and this would have come as no surprise to Hamilton Deane who had received two enquiries from America by 11.30am on the morning after its debut in Derby!

Of course, the next natural progression was for Dracula to move onto the silver screen – and as mentioned at the start of the article - there have been countless films made. Nevertheless, each and every one of those films can trace their origins back to the stage adaptation and that my friends, began in Derby.

Issue 5 - The Plague Village - The story of the selfless sacrifice made by the people of a Derbyshire village.

I remember very well where I was on the evening of March 23, 2020 and even if the date isn't immediately recognisable, you probably do too. It was then that the nation was put under lockdown for the first time in the COVID 19 pandemic. It was inevitable that this would happen as some point as the virus began to spread in the UK and throughout the world, but for one Derbyshire village it wasn't the first time that a pandemic had resulted in a lockdown.

The village was Eyam, and the year was 1666, but on this occasion, it wasn't a government-imposed lockdown. The villagers had quarantined themselves.

The story begins in 1665 when Alexander Hadfield, the local tailor, received a flea-infested bundle of cloth from London. His assistant George Viccars noticed that within a week, the bundle was damp and he opened it up to investigate. Before long he was dead and soon after the members of his household died too. Bubonic plague had arrived in Eyam.

A contemporary illustration of people fleeing the plague in London and in turn spreading it to other areas of the country.

The plague - known as the Black Death during the 14th Century when it caused an estimated 50 million deaths - had brought death and despair to England on various occasions before. The first outbreak in England had occurred between 1348 and 1350 when it killed around 30 to 40% of the population with further epidemics breaking out in 1563, 1593, 1625 and of course 1665.

From September 1665 to December of the same year, 42 villagers had already died in the outbreak – to put this into perspective the population stood at around 350 before the outbreak – and as spring came around in 1666 many villagers were considering fleeing the village to save both their lives and livelihoods.

It was at this point that William Mompesson intervened.

William was the newly appointed rector at Eyam and, wanting to stop the plague spreading to nearby towns, believed that the town of Eyam should be quarantined. Aside from the huge task of getting the villagers to agree to this sacrifice, there was another issue facing William because he was very unpopular with the residents of Eyam who preferred the previous rector who had been exiled to the edge of the village.

The previous rector in Eyam had been a man by the name of Thomas Stanley. Thomas – and most of his parish – had supported Oliver Cromwell and his Puritan government, prior to the restoration of the monarchy in 1660. When Thomas had refused to accept the 1662 Act of Uniformity - an Act introduced by Charles II which made it compulsory to use the Book of Common Prayer in religious services – he had been removed from the position and William had taken over in April 1664.

Realising he needed help, William personally met with and spoke to Thomas and between them they devised a plan and on June 24, 1666 Mompesson spoke to his parishioners.

Telling them that the Earl of Devonshire, who lived at nearby Chatsworth. had offered food and supplies if the village agreed to quarantined, he told them nobody should be allowed to either leave or enter the village. It was a sacrifice that he was prepared to make himself too, as he stated he would rather die himself than see other communities nearby decimated like theirs had been. Though the villagers were understandably hesitant, Thomas also stated his support for the plan and the villagers reluctantly agreed.

As well as the quarantine itself, various other measures were introduced. Families were to bury their own dead, church services were relocated to the natural amphitheatre of Cucklett Delph and supplies from surrounding villages would be left on marked rocks. When the villagers collected the supplies, they would make holes in the rock which they would fill with vinegar to disinfect the money left as payment.

While the villagers lived under these conditions the plague was contained – but its toll on the village was unfathomable.

Mary Hadfield was the sole survivor of the five household members who lived in this cottage.

By August 1666 five to six people were dying daily and entire families were decimated. In the space of eight days Elizabeth Hancock buried six of her children and her husband, while Mary Hadfield – wife of Alexander Hadfield the tailor – lost thirteen relatives including Alexander himself, and by the time the plague abated in November 1666, only 83 people had survived.

Though William Mompesson survived his wife Catherine did not.

William stayed in Eyam for three further years helping to rebuild the shattered community before being relieved of his post and transferred to the parish of Eakring.

The plan of William, the support of Thomas Stanley and the consent of the villagers was truly an incredibly selfless act that protected nearby towns such as Sheffield and Bakewell and is still commemorated at the annual Plague Commemoration service, held on the last Sunday of August in Cucklet Delf, the place where Mompesson held his outdoor services three and a half centuries ago.

For more information on Eyam go to: www.eyamvillage.org.uk/

Issue 5 - Rykneld Bowling Club - A beautifully peaceful and serene oasis of tranquility

If we travel back to 1918 in England, we find a country very much still at war during what became known to us as World War One. It wouldn't be until November of that year that Germany would sign the Armistice at Compiègne, ending the war, but back at home people were trying to live their lives as best they could in the shadow of the war, and leisure and entertainment activities played a large part in that.

It was in that very same field of leisure activities over at the Arboretum Bowling Club that a row that had been brewing was about to boil over. Various members of the club had become disaffected by the way it was run and matters came to a head when they left the club to form their own. The new club was Rykneld Bowling Club and though it took more than a year before games commenced at Farley Drive, which is now Farley Road, the club was formed on February 26 1918.

It is believed that the dispute had centred around a desire to adopt some new rules concerning the use of their green and twelve of the members – all important businesspeople in Derby at the time – felt strongly enough about it to leave the club and form their own. A bank loan was secured and a piece of land was purchased from the Rykneld Estate for £653 – around £30,000 in today's money – and the green was built. With a railway carriage purchased to provide shelter at the side of the green – the purpose-built club house which remains today, did not arrive until the mid-1930s – the club opened its doors on May 10, 1919 and, with 100 members already signed up, they played their first game.

Over the years the club has seen some notable names from Derby's history play there. In bygone days it was customary for the town's mayor to send down the first wood of a new season and other dignitaries such as Colonel Horatio Rawlings – the Chief Constable of Derby from 1926 to 1956 - were also regular visitors.

Jimmy Hagan – a divine footballing talent who was inexplicably sold by Derby County to Sheffield United in 1938 - played at the club whenever he came to visit his old friend, veteran athlete Lew Patrick, who was a keen Rykneld member. Hagan was subject to a bid that would have been a British record transfer fee of £32,500 from Sheffield Wednesday in February 1951 before declining the move, and went on to lead Benfica to three successive league titles in

Portugal as a manager with one of those successes boasting an undefeated league campaign. He enjoyed a lifelong friendship with the legendary Eusébio that began at Benfica.

Though over the years Derby has sadly lost some famous bowling venues including the greens at the rear of pubs such as the Coach and Horses on Mansfield Road and the former Mafeking Hotel in Porter Road, Rykneld Bowling Club has over the years always prided itself on its self-sufficiency. In 2008 the club raised £10,000 to refurbish and improve the club house including the installation of disabled access and facilities enabling it to be used by other organisations in the area, as well as organising a new roof and a new kitchen. Alongside the floodlights which arrived in the 1980s the club boasts a wonderful venue.

The clubhouse at Rykneld Bowling Club.

Though bordered by two very busy thoroughfares in Manor Road and Burton Road you'd have no idea or sense of this once you step inside the club. It's a beautifully peaceful and serene oasis of tranquility in an ever-busy world and the love and care put into its maintenance and upkeep is easy to see. Now 105 years old and counting, the club has a wonderful past to look back upon and a bright future to look forward to.

Rykneld Bowling Club can be found at:

39 Farley Road, Derby DE23 6BW

www.rykneldbowlingclub.co.uk

Issue 5 - "To avoid bad company" - The true story of a man who escaped the hangman once...but not twice.

I believe that the further back we travel in time, the more difficult it is to put ourselves into someone else's shoes.

Life was so different the further back we go, with poverty much more severe and widespread and people's everyday lives and motivations were influenced by the harsher environment in which they lived.

That being said, I'd still like to think that if one of our ancestors came incredibly close to being executed, they'd learn a lesson from it and try their hardest to never be in that situation again.

Of course, the whole point of this article is that on occasions this assumption would be wrong. In the case of Thomas Hopkinson, very wrong indeed.

If we were able to travel back in time to 1817 and take a look inside the County Gaol on Friar Gate in Derby, we'd find amongst the prisoners five men - John Brown, Thomas Jackson, George Booth, John King and the subject of this article, Thomas Hopkinson. The five men in question had been accused of setting fire to hay and corn stacks in South Wingfield at the property of Winfield Halton. It was one of the many offences punishable by death during the latter part of what was known as the Bloody Code - a series of laws in England, Wales and Ireland in the 18th and early 19th centuries which mandated the death penalty for a wide range of crimes.

Four of the men would be hanged for the crime on August 15, 1817 but Thomas was spared the hangman's noose. Though the Derby Mercury detailed on July 24, 1817 that all five men would go to the Assizes and face this charge, the report on the sentencing seven days later omitted to mention Thomas.

The explanation was simple enough - showing an instinct for survival that belied his later mistakes, Thomas had turned King's Evidence. To turn King's Evidence the accused would admit their guilt and testify against their associates or accomplices, often in exchange for leniency in sentencing or immunity from prosecution. It seemed in this case that Thomas was acquitted while his erstwhile associates were launched into eternity. Thomas, it is believed, was suspicious that John King was intending to turn King's Evidence himself - at one point he had made a confession which he then retracted - and decided to get there first.

The site of Derby's County Gaol in 2023 – Photo by Jamie Turner.

Notably at the execution, and despite the fact that they were soon to die, three of the four men - when confronted by a heavy downpour on their way to the gallows - chose to shelter from it. The Derby Mercury described how "two of them deliberately retreated to the shelter of an umbrella which was expanded on the drop, and a third placed himself under cover of the door way. The inconvenience of being wet was felt and avoided by men who knew that they had not five minutes longer to live!!"

Thomas was eighteen years old at this time and contemporary literature – which must be said held a certain degree of bias against him – described him as someone who, once he had entered a life of crime, had abandoned 'every moral feeling and every religious consideration'.

He had been born in Ashover and lived with this father until the age of fourteen. At that point the family moved to Woolley Moor and here he had 'formed an intercourse with abandoned companions and commenced that profligate career which brought him to his untimely end'.

He had formed a close association with Thomas Jackson who was described at the time as being 'wicked company'. Hopkinson's nights were spent 'poaching, robbing hen roosts, gardens, and barns' and his days 'were spent either in that kind of idleness which is ever the fruitful source of fresh crimes or in dissipating, in profligate excess, the money acquired by his nefarious practices'.

Though this lifestyle came to an end for four of the five at the end of a rope, and though you might have hoped that this was a wake-up call for Thomas, he continued his criminal career unabashed.

Though his previous associates and companions had been hanged, Thomas made fresh acquaintances and amongst these was a young man called John Fletcher. It was in 1819 that the now twenty-year-old Thomas, alongside John Fletcher, committed highway robbery on the turnpike road near Dronfield. Their victim was a man by the name of William Bucknall and he was described as being put 'in bodily fear' whilst they stole a 'purse containing twelve shillings and six-pence'.

In February of that year both Hopkinson and Fletcher were arrested for the crime. Though Hopkinson had confessed to an entire litany of crimes whilst incarcerated, he steadfastly proclaimed his innocence to the latest charge of highway robbery. Regardless of this, both he and Fletcher were both found guilty and sentenced to death. Though on occasions whilst held in the gaol, Hopkinson had a tendency to suddenly launch into humorously indecent songs, he was generally regarded to have shown quite a high level of bravado considering the circumstances that he was found in. The Derby Mercury described it rather cuttingly as 'what might have been anticipated from one lost to all moral sensibility, and so accustomed to vice as scarcely to have preserved the distinctions between right and wrong'.

It is possible that he was quite hopeful of a reprieve. On the day that he had been sentenced to death, Hopkinson and Fletcher were just two of seventeen prisoners who had received the death sentence at the Assizes that day. Ultimately fifteen of those people, including John Fletcher, were reprieved. Only Hopkinson and Hannah Bocking – a sixteen-year-old girl found guilty of murder – went on to face the executioner with all hopes of a reprieve dashed. It was the sight of Hannah Bocking seated in the condemned pew of the gaol chapel only an hour before her execution, that caused one of only two occasions on which Hopkinson's bravado faltered. The other occasion had been when he had broken down and cried when his father visited him on the day of his execution.

On the morning of his execution on April 2, 1819, Hopkinson also took part in the usual religious observations whilst spending time with the chaplain. He expressed his 'free forgiveness' for all his enemies and said he hoped that 'his example would prove a warning to those who should witness his execution'. When asked what his warning to young people would be in order to prevent them from falling into a life of crime, his reply was simply 'to avoid bad company'.

His death on the gallows was neither quick nor painless, with the Derby Mercury reporting that he was 'much convulsed after the drop fell' and that 'he seemed to suffer more than is usual on such occasions'.

Though we don't know the name of the executioner that day, in all surety we do know of someone it might have been – the father of Thomas Jackson who had witnessed Hopkinson turning King's Evidence on his son two years previously and the subsequent execution of him. The father had volunteered to be the one to execute him but the Derby Mercury's coverage of this was somewhat ambiguous as to whether the offer had been accepted - whilst being quite definitive as to what they thought of the offer in either event. Referring to the man as a 'wretch', they wrote that 'human nature recoils with horror from such a monster, and rejoices to hope that this may be a solitary instance of such depravity'.

Ultimately, we will never know if the offer was accepted – although as John Crossland once hung his own father and brother in Derby to avoid the hangman himself, we can see that impromptu hangmen were well within the scope of possibilities – but either way the life of Thomas was brought to an end.

Issue 5 – "Before his time limited" – Executed for returning home early from transportation.

If I could give anybody any advice when it comes to researching local history – not that you're under any obligation to follow it of course – it would be learning to accept that no matter how much you dig and search, there will be some things you might never find out or know.

Of course, it is the gems that you find after extensive research and hard toil that makes the failures easier to bear, but at the same time, I really did have to accept when I researched this piece that I'd probably never find out anything substantial about the person who was Thomas Hulley.

The irony is that when I started work on this piece I wasn't originally searching for information about Thomas Hulley. I was looking for a true story that I could use to show how the local newspapers of old – specifically the Derby Mercury - reported local events.

I'd searched various events from our past for something suitable – from extreme weather to execution reports – before my eyes were caught by a line of text that I'd read various times before for other research projects.

11. Thomas Hulley, for returning from transportation, 1757.

The line was always number 11 in a list of executions in Derby from 1732 onwards, that the Derby Mercury often printed when reporting on the latest addition to the list, and this time I resolved to find out more about this event.

The first mention I found of Thomas was in the Derby Mercury in August 1754. There was no article specifically about him, merely a brief paragraph in a report on the Derby Assizes from August 14 of that year.

> And Thomas Hulley, for feloniously breaking into the Shop of Samuel and Jonathan Hodgkinfons, of Baflow, and taking and carrying away feveral Pieces of dreft Leather, &c. being convicted thereof was ordered to be tranfported for feven Years.

Thomas had been convicted of stealing several pieces of dressed leather from a shop in Baslow and he'd been sentenced to be transported for seven years. In many ways Thomas had, I suppose, been lucky. It wasn't uncommon for people to be hanged for stealing – thirteen years before William Elliott had suffered that fate in Derby – but being transported was still no easy ride.

Though many people generally associate convicts being transported to Australia, before 1776 convicts sentenced to transportation were sent to North America and the West Indies. Thanks to the sterling work of Anne Bull – her work on transportation can be found at www.derby.gov.uk/derbyhistory – it was easy enough to find out that Thomas had been sent to North America.

Transported convicts were often chained up by leg irons on board convict ships, and with conditions on the journey often cramped, some convicts died on the way. Once they arrived, they were put to hard physical work and it was not uncommon for a convict to be whipped and punished if they disobeyed rules.

Within three years - as we can see from the Derby Mercury on March 25, 1757 – Thomas had escaped his sentence, returned back to England and had been caught and sentenced for his crime. This time the sentence was death. He was one of two people to receive the death penalty at the Assizes in that session. The other was Thomas Ratcliff.

> This Evening the Affizes ended here on the Crown Side, when two Perfons received Sentence of Death, viz. Thomas Hulley, for returning from Tranfportation before his Time limited, being try'd here in Auguft, 1754, for breaking into the Shop of Mr. Hodgkinfon of Biflow, and carrying away feveral Pieces of drefs'd Leather, and then order'd to be tranfported for feven Years : And Thomas Ratcliff, (remov'd from Nottingham) for ftealing a Black Mare from Robert Hartfhorn, of Rofton in this County, the 10th of February laft, as advertis'd in this Paper.

Within a week – as we can see in this excerpt from the Derby Mercury – Thomas Ratcliff had already received a reprieve and by the tone of the article it seemed that a reprieve was quite likely a possibility for Thomas Hulley too.

> *Derby, April* 7. Thomas Ratcliff, condemn'd at the Assizes held here last Week, for stealing a Mare, was reprieved before Mr. Justice Bathurst left this Place; but Thomas Hulley, condemn'd also for returning from Transportation before the Expiration of his Time, still continues under Sentence, but it is generally reported that a Petition will be presented to the King in his Favour.

As you can see, nothing that was reported at the time gave any indication to just who Thomas was as an individual. Every time it was a simple factual update on the situation. A week later the next factual update was something that Thomas surely hoped fell under the heading of 'no news is good news'.

> *Derby, April* 14. We don't hear that any Answer has yet been receiv'd, to the Petition sent up last Week, in favour of Thomas Hulley, condemn'd at our last Assizes for returning from Transportation.

Sadly however, in this instance it wasn't the case. Later that month, on April 22, 1757, the newspaper printed the update that his attempted reprieve had been unsuccessful.

> We are inform'd, that the Execution of Thomas Hulley, condemn'd at our last Assizes for returning from Transportation, is now certainly fix'd for To-morrow. This poor unfortunate Man's Case is generally pitied, having by his good Behaviour, ever since his Confinement, given good hopes of a Reformation, had he been saved; for which purpose repeated Applications were made; and tho' not attended with the desired Success, yet he received the Appointment for his Execution with great Composure, and only desired he might not be carried in a Cart, but walk to the Place of Execution, attended by the Minister; and that a Coffin might be provided for him, as he had it not in his Power to buy one.

Perhaps the request for a coffin gave an indication for his motive for his initial crime of stealing. Many people in that era lived a life of poverty. Ultimately, we will never truly know, as we will probably never know anything else about Thomas the person.

A simple paragraph in the paper told the last we know of his story. It wasn't even original copy from the Derby Mercury – they'd reprinted it from the London Gazette.

Derby, May 5. Laſt Friday Thomas Hulley was executed here, purſuant to his Sentence. He walked to the Place of Execution, attended by the Rev. Mr. Blackwell, and behav'd as became one in his melancholy Circumſtances; but ſaid very little to the Publick.

Issue 5 - War on the doorstep. - When death and destruction arrived in Derby

In 1982 I was nine years old and attended Firs Estate Junior School. The school itself was no more than five minutes away from my house, so every day I came home for my lunch before returning back to school for my afternoon lessons.

It was one particular lunchtime as I walked through the back door and into the kitchen that I got hurriedly shushed by my mother. She was listening intently to the radio until she eventually explained that we were now at war with Argentina in what became known as the Falklands War. I followed the news of the war as best I could at that age, and I was struck by how far away everything was happening and wondered what it must be like for those who actually lived there.

It all felt very far away again a few years later when I was 17 and the Gulf War was beamed live to our TVs, but again I wondered what it would feel like if a seemingly far away war suddenly got closer to home. The other day I came across an article regarding the Zeppelin air raid on Derby in World War One and a thought formed in my head.

What must it have been like to realise that a far away war might now suddenly be on your doorstep?

World War One had commenced – from a British perspective - on August 4, 1914 but it wasn't until 1916 that Derby, for the very first time, saw the death and destruction of the war arrive squarely on its doorstep.

German Zeppelins had begun their attacks on England in 1915 and over the course of that year and the following year there had been 52 raids which had killed 556 people and injured 1,357. However, it was just after midnight on February 1, 1916 that the terror of the Zeppelin bombs hit Derby.

The Zeppelin in question was lost and under the command of Captain Alois Boeker. It was part of multiple airships that had intended to attack Liverpool and Birmingham. Zeppelins however were slow and lumbering and not one of them had got nearer to Liverpool than Stoke before beginning to turn back.

It was whilst one of the airships was over Derby just after midnight that it dispatched its remaining 21 high explosive bombs and four incendiaries at nine various locations on the south side of the town.

A Zeppelin Bomber.

The town had received warning about a possible impending air raid just after 7pm the previous evening. Measures such as dousing street lighting, halting tramcars and closing businesses had been quickly enacted and when three airships passed close by shortly after it was thought that the precautions had been successful. Confidence in their success lead to the measures being relaxed just before midnight with the resulting light convincing Captain Boeker that he had reached Liverpool. He therefore released his bombs.

Four men died when nine high explosive bombs were dropped near to the No 9 Shed of the Loco Works - 32-year-old fitter William Bancroft of Strutt Street, 23-year-old Henry Hithersay of Devonshire Street and 54-year-old engine driver James Gibbs Hardy, also of Strutt Street, died that night with 48-year-old fitter Charles Henry Champion of Fleet Street dying three days later from his injuries. A Mrs Constantine – a former schoolmistress - who lived nearby, also died that night of a heart attack during the raid.

Five bombs were also dropped on the Carriage and Wagon Works, three bombs - two high-explosive and one incendiary - fell near to the gasworks on what is now Pride Park, while other bombs landed on the corner of Bateman Street, the Metalite Lamp Works on Graham Road, Fletcher's Lace Mill on Osmaston Road and on Horton Street.

With their full quota of bombs dispatched, Captain Boeker and his crew returned home for a debriefing at which they reported – mistakenly - that they had bombed Liverpool.

On February 3, the Derby Daily Telegraph reported that across England 33 men, 20 women and six children had been killed in the raids.

Derby would again be bombed in World War Two, but this was perhaps the first time in centuries that war had truly presented itself on our doorsteps.

Issue 6 - Hanging in chains - The story of the gibbet and two macabre cases of its use in Derby and Derbyshire

You'd think – if you looked back through the sands of time – that even in an era where people's lives were a hard and harsh struggle, being sentenced to death by hanging would be pretty much the worst thing that could happen to you.

You'd be wrong to think this as it turns out – if you were particularly unlucky, things could get even worse than this. You could, after all, be executed in an era where post-mortem punishment was the norm under the Murder Act of 1752.

The Murder Act of 1752, in an attempt to be 'better preventing the horrid crime of murder' included a provision that 'in no case whatsoever shall the body of any murderer be suffered to be buried' and mandated either dissection or the 'hanging in chains' of the cadaver as the alternatives.

Looking through the eyes of the people of that era, being denied a 'decent burial' was seen as much worse than simply being executed. The Murder Act, however, showed no mercy in these regards, explicitly stating that this was in order to add 'some further terror and peculiar mark of infamy' to the death sentence and to 'impress a just horror in the mind of the offender, and on the minds of such as shall be present, of the heinous crime of murder'.

The hanging of the cadaver in chains – or gibbetting – had existed before the 1752 Murder Act, but the Act regularised the practice and in the history of our county there are two notable stories connected to this.

The first story dates back to the murder of Mary Vickers in 1774 in Full Street, Derby. The murder occurred during a burglary committed by Matthew Cocklayne and George Foster. Though both men fled to Ireland and carried on with their criminal ways, Foster was ultimately shot in the head during a robbery and Cocklayne was captured. Upon his capture it was found out that he was wanted in Derby and he was returned there to stand trial where he was found guilty and sentenced to death by hanging. His execution took place on March 21st, 1776.

After he had been hanged, his body was firstly taken down and coated in a preserving tar which would enable the corpse to remain intact for longer. His body was then placed in a gibbet, and it was hung on Bradshaw Hay – near to the present-day Bradshaw Way.

Corpses displayed like this were often left there for many years. Cocklayne's corpse had already been there for fifteen years when a young man casually wandered into the town centre of Derby brandishing his skull with The Derby Mercury reporting that:

Full Street in c.1760 by S. H. Parkins – fourteen years before the murder of Mary Vickers.

A lad was met coming into this town, having in his hand the skull of Matthew Cocklane, who was executed on the 21st of March, 1776, for the murder of Mrs. Vickars, and afterwards hung in chains: It seems that the wind had blown him from his exalted situation the preceding night."

Though it would be nice to think that older and wiser heads had corrected him on his behaviour, it transpired that others then headed off to get a piece of the corpse with the report stating:

His hair, skin, and most of his bones were in high preservation; numbers – who had often stood in melancholy gaze, repaired to the gibbet, and returned with various parts of his remains."

Between 1752 and 1832, 134 men were gibbetted in England. It was formally abolished in 1834.

Of course, as much as it may be hard to believe, there was something even worse than being executed and then gibbetted and this was to be gibbetted alive – a fate which, it is alleged, befell a beggar in the 17th century in Baslow, near Chatsworth Park. As the story goes, he'd been going from house to house begging and had arrived at the house of a lady after smelling bacon cooking.

He asked for some – only to be told it was all gone. When he asked for any other food and was again declined, he forced his way into the property in anger and forced the boiling bacon fat down her throat, killing her.

This all obviously caused a commotion, and he was arrested immediately for his crime and put in the gibbet alive and left to die. Now as he was alive, he wouldn't have been tarred so he would have slowly starved to death before the birds came to peck at his flesh.

Gibbet Moor – the location of a beggars gruesome live-gibbeting.

Legends say that it was the sounds of the man's begging, screaming, and pleading – heard by the Duke of Devonshire – that caused the Duke to use his influence to put an end to live gibbetting in England and the location of the gibbet is still to this day known as Gibbet Moor.

Issue 6 – "For most conspicuous bravery" - The story of a young Derby man and his selfless sacrifice in World War One.

When the overwhelming majority of Bridge Gate in Derby was swept away in the 1960s to make way for the building of the inner ring road the bulldozers, as they have a habit of doing, swept away not just the bricks and mortar of the buildings but also certain locations that are tied to historically important figures from Derby's past. Nothing was truer than this when – during the ring road development – they demolished No 4, Court 12, Wide Yard which lay just off Bridge Gate itself.

No 4 was a property that had seen the birth of not just a historical figure from Derby's past, but a true and selfless hero – the person in question was Private Jacob Rivers.

Jacob was born at No 4 on November 17, 1881 to George and Adeline Rivers. Jacob was one of seven children and when Jacob's father died aged of forty-one, he and his brothers – when they were old enough to find work – all sought it out to ease the financial burden on their mother.

Private Jacob Rivers VC.

Jacob joined the Royal Scottish Fusiliers in 1899 and saw seven years of military service in India and Burma. He was discharged in 1907 and was placed on the military reserve and on his return to Derby he found work as a labourer with the Midland Railway.

Jacob was one of the first men to volunteer when World War One began in 1914 and this time joined the Sherwood Foresters. With prior and extensive military experience, Jacob was one of the first draft of men to be sent to France in 1915 and it was here – in March 1915 – that Jacob was involved in the Battle of Neuve Chapelle. It was a battle that would result in more than 11,000 Allied soldiers being killed, wounded or missing.

The offensive began on March 10 with Rivers 'battalion held in reserve, but it was brought into action the following day when it was ordered to the village of Pietre.

Jacob's battalion soon found their advance halted by machine gun posts and had to dig in. The next day, however, they found themselves under considerable pressure on their right flank. To relieve the pressure Jacob cautiously approached the German position and threw several bombs on them causing them to retire and helping relieve the pressure on his battalion.

Incredibly Jacob didn't just do this once. He repeated the act later the same day again causing the Germans to retire. This time he was killed doing it.

For his actions, he was awarded the Victoria Cross (VC). The VC is the highest and most prestigious decoration of the British honours system and is awarded for valour in the presence of the enemy. The citation for this award – published in the London Gazette on April 28, 1915 read:

For most conspicuous bravery at Neuve-Chapelle on 12th March, 1915, when he, on his own initiative, crept to within a few yards of a very large number of the enemy who were massed on the flank of an advanced company of his battalion, and hurled bombs on them. His action caused the enemy to retire, and so relieved the situation. Pte. Rivers performed a second act of great bravery on the same day, similar to the first mentioned, again causing the enemy to retire. He was killed on this occasion.

With the fighting so fierce it was impossible to retrieve Jacob's body and so one of Derby's greatest heroes has no known grave, though his name is commemorated on the Le Touret Memorial.

Jacob's mother received the VC on her son's behalf in October 1915. In a letter signed by the King it read:

"It is with much satisfaction that I convey to you the Victoria Cross awarded to the late Private Jacob Rivers.

"I deeply regret that his death deprived me of the pride of personally conferring upon him this, the greatest of all military distinctions."

Issue 6 - Are you prepared to die for your doctrine? - The tragic story and brutal end of Joan Waste

I'm sure amongst you – our readers – there will be people who either have a disability or know someone who has. In my case my fiancée is what we now term as severely sight impaired. That's not to say she has no vision at all, but the vision she does have is bad – very bad. She – as she does with everything – shows immense bravery with the everyday struggles she faces and the support she's received from both the council and the health service has been invaluable. It has, however, often made me wonder how people coped with such disabilities in the days before such support was available, and the further we go back in time the more pertinent the question gets.

If we go back to the 1500s in Derby, we find a young woman who coped admirably with her blindness – Joan Waste. She was also, by all accounts, a very kind and caring individual but neither her kindness nor bravery would save her from a brutal and unfair death when she was burned at the stake in 1556.

Joan Waste had been born blind in 1534 to William Waste and his wife Joan. Though blind, Joan seemed to be a determined person and by the age of twelve she had learned to knit as well as make ropes alongside her rope-maker father.

Joan was also a devout and practicing Christian and was herself a Protestant - a form of Christianity that originated with the 16th-century Reformation, a movement against what its followers perceived to be errors in the Catholic Church. She attended mass at St. Peter's Church in Derby. The fact she was a Protestant was initially of no concern whatsoever until Queen Mary I came to the throne in 1553. Mary was vigorous in her attempts to reverse the Reformation and in January 1555 it was made illegal by Parliament to hold Protestant views.

Joan's Protestant views were well known in the town. She had worked hard and saved to buy her own copy of the bible. Needing someone to read it regularly to her, she finally found a man called John Hurt who happily agreed to help.

Hurt was in the Derby Gaol at the time for failure to pay his debts. Described as a 'sober, grave man' it seems that Hurt was one of many people imprisoned at the time for their 'failure' to get out of poverty. Joan had taken it upon herself from an early age to visit the prisoners in the gaol and Hurt was happy to make her acquaintance and to read to her until illness made him unable to do it anymore. Determined as ever, she asked friends to read to her for a penny a time.

By the time of her last year on earth – 1556 – mass was now being read in Latin as per the instructions of Queen Mary I and Joan objected to this. She also refused to accept the doctrine of transubstantiation - the belief in the conversion of the communion bread and wine into the body and blood of Christ at consecration - maintaining they were still bread and wine and merely symbolic.

Joan and her family attended services at St. Peter's in Derby.

With Joan steadfast in her Protestant beliefs, it was inevitable that a clash would occur with the authorities and in June 1556 she was called in front of the Diocesan Bishop, Ralph Baine and his Chancellor, Dr Anthony Draycott to defend her views.

Her trial took place at what was then All Saints Parish Church – now Derby Cathedral. At her trial Joan, whilst answering her charges, made it clear that she was aware of several people who had been imprisoned, tortured and killed for their beliefs.

She said: *"Are you prepared to die for your doctrine? If not, then for God's sake trouble me no more. I am but a poor, blind, uneducated woman, but with God's help I am ready to yield up my life in this faith."*

With the Bishop and the Chancellor growing increasingly angry, they tried to persuade her to agree with the doctrine of transubstantiation and threatened her with imprisonment, torture and death if she refused to do so. In response, Joan asked the Bishop if he really believed in his heart that his doctrine was true, and if he was, therefore, willing to answer for her on the Day of Judgement

The Bishop replied that he did and he would, only to back down when the Chancellor said:

"My Lord, you do not know what you are doing - you may, under no circumstances, answer to God for a heretic."

Telling Joan she needed to acquiesce and that she would need to answer to God on her own account, she replied:

"If you refuse to take on your conscience as true what you wish me to believe, I will answer you no more; do your pleasure."

Joan was remanded to the bailiffs in Derby and placed in gaol where around five weeks later she received the news that she would be burnt as a heretic.

On the day of her execution – August 1 – she was taken first to All Saints Church where the Chancellor himself preached the sermon. He began by telling the congregation:

This woman is condemned for denying the Sacrament of the Altar to be the very body and blood of Christ, really and substantially and is, for this reason, cut off from the body of the Catholic Church."

He went on to say that:

"She is not only blind in her bodily eyes, but also blind in the eyes of her soul. And as her body will soon be consumed with material fire, so her soul will be burned in Hell with everlasting fire, as soon as it is separated from the body. There it will remain, world without end."

After he had forbidden anyone to pray for her, Joan was taken to her place of execution holding her brother's hand all the way there.

Windmill Hill Pit – the site of Joan's execution – pictured here in the 19th century.

Joan was burned at the stake at Windmill Hill Pit which lay where Lime Avenue – off Burton Road – is now. Whilst the flame consumed her, the Chancellor – who hadn't attended the execution – returned to his inn, ate and then slept.

Issue 6 - William Hutton - The journey of one man from abject poverty to well-earned success.

Regular readers of Derby Uncovered will have seen from time to time in our publication, mentions of William Hutton, the Derby-born historian whose book - '*The History of Derby From The Remote Ages of Antiquity to 1791*' – is still used to this day by countless fellow historians, both professional and amateur.

For those who haven't read the book, and those who may not have heard of him, you will have walked past his statue countless times – perhaps without realising it – because it is one of the four statues on the side of the old Boots Building at the junction of East Street and St. Peter's Street.

But just who was William Hutton? It's easy to assume that he came from a background of noble scholars due to his literary feats, but if you made that assumption, you'd be wrong.

Very wrong indeed.

William Hutton.

William was born into poverty in Full Street, Derby, on September 30, 1723. His father was a woolcomber by trade, though often he was without work. A regular of the ale-house, his father had squandered a successful start in life with his hard-earned apprenticeship and exhibited a lack of application and effort once married. As a result of this, the level of poverty that William experienced as a child – a level which got worse upon the death of his mother in 1733 – was something that he never, ever forgot.

In his autobiography, William mentions that there were many occasions that he, alongside his mother and his siblings, ate nothing at all. "At one time", says Hutton, "I fasted from breakfast one day to noon the next" before he ate a hastily-made pudding of flour and water.

Though his school life was short and inadequate, he was at least taught to read by his father but with a father who also believed in physical punishments, Hutton's early years were not just full of poverty but were also an extremely harsh environment.

From the age of seven he began to work at the Silk Mill in Derby from 5am in the morning till 7pm in the evening and for his first year there he was too small to even reach the machines and had to wear a pair of pattens – overshoes that are somewhat similar to clogs – to enable him to do so.

Working at the mill was, in itself, a brutal experience for him. In later life he often referred to the 'ignorance and vulgarity' of the mill-hands and the slightest mistake from any of the children working there could result in a physical beating. Hutton himself was beat so hard with a cane on one occasion that the scar it left remained with him, both physically and mentally, for the rest of his life.

He was to spend seven years at the mill before he left and moved to Nottingham where he spent another seven years to a stockinger. During this period, he would often visit Derby for a few days and after one visit, at Christmas 1745, he began to bind and repair old books. In 1749, when he had decided to adopt this trade full-time, he walked from Nottingham to London and back again to purchase the tools required. He performed both legs of the journey within nine days – it seems long walks were a forte for Hutton as he is also regarded to be the first person in modern times to walk the entire length of Hadrian's Wall - and in 1750 he settled in Birmingham where he established himself as a bookbinder and bookseller.

In 1755, Hutton married Sarah Cock from Aston-on-Trent and they had three sons and a daughter. In 1756 Hutton opened a paper warehouse – the first in Birmingham – which became profitable. Now freed from his childhood poverty, he built a country house on Bennetts Hill in Washwood Heath and bought a house in High Street.

Amongst the various book he wrote, Hutton published his History of Birmingham in 1782 and his History of Derby in 1791 and during his later life visited Derby on occasional intervals. During one of these visits in 1803, he found out that every person he had known at the Silk Mill had now passed away.

The Silk Mill where William worked – painted in 1776 by Moses Griffiths.

Hutton died in 1815 and at the time was perhaps never truly valued by the town of his birth – his legacy, however, remains with us to this day.

This author still uses his book regularly whilst writing for Derby Uncovered. If you remember the story of the daredevil, the tight rope, the Cathedral tower and the donkey or indeed the gruesome tale of John Crossland executing his own father and brother to avoid the hangman himself, you can thank William Hutton for both of them – that was the original source material I used.

It's not just his writing though, that I believe we should thank William Hutton for. It's the inspiration he gives us when we learn how he overcame an incredibly poor and harsh start in life to become one of the greatest historians this city has ever had.

If you enjoyed this, then why not subscribe to our bi-monthly Derby Uncovered Newspaper?

Full of the very best of Derby and Derbyshire's history and heritage, it's completely free to subscribe – you only pay the postage and packaging.

Go to www.derbyshire-bazaar.com to subscribe now.

Would you like your story to be published?

All of us at Derby Uncovered believe firmly that the history of our area is created by and belongs to you - the people of the area.

We want to help you tell your stories and your history and to help us do that we have now launched our book publishing service.

Our aim is to print and publish the stories, lives, and histories that you – the people of Derby and Derbyshire - have to tell.

You don't have to be a professional author - you just need to have an interesting story to tell. If you'd like to find out more about this, then please get in touch.

Want to make a difference to the future of Derby?

Derby Uncovered Community Interest Company has been formed with the aim of revitalising city-centre properties within the Cathedral Quarter.

To see how you can help please visit:

www.derbyuncoveredcic.org

Though every effort has been made to make sure that we have not used any copyrighted images in this book, please feel free to contact us if you feel that we have. Our books are printed on a print-on-demand basis which permits us the opportunity to remove any erroneous images immediately.

www.derbyuncovered.com

@derbyuncovered

Printed in Great Britain
by Amazon